THE CROSS STITCHER'S BIBLE

Fabulous Flowers

Jane Greenoff

David and Charles

To Bill, my husband and best friend

A DAVID & CHARLES BOOK
Copyright © David & Charles Limited 2006

David & Charles is an F+W Publications Inc. company
4700 East Galbraith Road
Cincinnati, OH 45236

First published in the UK in 2006

Text and designs copyright © Jane Greenoff 2006

ISBN 13: 978-0-7153-2193-5
ISBN 10: 0-7153-2193-5

Printed in UK by Butler & Tanner Ltd
for David & Charles
Brunel House   Newton Abbot   Devon

Executive Editor Cheryl Brown
Editor Jennifer Proverbs
Project Editor   Linda Clements
Art Editor/Designer Prudence Rogers
Production Controller Ros Napper
Photography Kim Sayer and Karl Adamson

Visit our website at www.davidandcharles.co.uk

David & Charles books are available from all good bookshops; alternatively you can contact
our Orderline on 0870 9908222 or write to us at FREEPOST EX2 110, D&C Direct, Newton
Abbot, TQ12 4ZZ (no stamp required UK only); US customers call 800-289-0963 and
Canadian customers call 800-840-5220.

Contents

Introduction 4
Back to Basics 6

Sensational Spring Flowers 10
Hardanger Tulip Bowl 10
Hardanger Coaster 10
Spring Flowers Sampler 13
Tiny Flowers Needlecase 13

Cottage Garden Blooms 18
Hollyhock and Bumblebees 18
Fluffy Bumblebee Card 18
Foxglove Garden Diary 20

Wonderful Wildflowers 24
Wildflower Stitch Sampler 24
Wildflower Chatelaine 24
Blue Harebell Poppet 26
Wildflower Charm Sampler 26
Poppy Hardanger Heart 28

Romantic Roses 32
Rich Red Rose 32
Rosebud Gift Card 32
Cross Stitch Rosa Vulgaris 35
Blackwork Rosa Vulgaris 35

Lovely Lilies 40
Orange Flame Lilies 40
Yellow Lily Scissor Pad 40
Day Lily Trio 42

Oriental Orchids 48
Hot Pink Orchid 48
Three Orchid Card 48
Bumblebee Orchid 50
Orchid Trinket Pot 52

Extravagant Exotics 56
Hummingbird and Hibiscus 56
Beaded Hummingbird Pincushion 56
Beaded Hibiscus Cushion 58
Frosted Amaryllis 58

Colourful Climbers 64
Clematis Trellis Cushion 64
Beaded Clematis Amulet 64
Passion Flower Purse 66
Morning Glory Glasses Case 68

Historical Flora 70
Jacobean Flower Bell Pull 70
Honeysuckle Notebook 70
Antique Flowers Cushion 72

Motif Library 76
Stitch Library 102
Making Up 113
Suppliers 119
Acknowledgments/About the Author 120
Index 121

Introduction

When *The Cross Stitcher's Bible* was first published in 2000 I was very pleased by its success, and even more so later when I saw well-used copies appearing from work boxes and stitching totes!

This is my second project book echoing the themes, technical know-how and information of *The Cross Stitcher's Bible* but this time featuring the ever-popular theme of flowers. As always, the problem with a book dedicated to flowers is what to include and what to leave out! There are so many glorious blooms to choose from but I hope you like my final selection and will find plenty of lovely things to stitch.

As with my previous books, I have included all the information you need to complete the projects, but I do recommend using *The Cross Stitcher's Bible* for a more detailed technical approach to some of the techniques. The book is packed with ideas: 34 detailed projects plus a further 126 designs in a Motif Library, beginning on page 76. Useful technique sections called Technique Focus are included throughout, explaining more complex techniques, with clear diagrams where necessary. Apart from the main projects, which have full stepped instructions, I have included some handmade cards and other

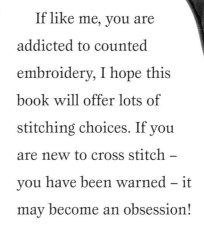

creative items using sections of the main charts. All of the stitches used are described and illustrated in the extensive Stitch Library beginning on page 102 and some of the stitches that were used in *The Cross Stitcher's Bible* are included here in an abbreviated form. Making up techniques, covered at the back of the book, show you how to finish and present your work beautifully.

I have been stitching using counted thread techniques for over 20 years and yet it still continues to fascinate me. I am still learning new techniques so I can tempt you into similar discoveries. I don't think I will ever tire of seeing a design grow on a piece of fabric and I know that I would feel quite lost without some linen and a needle poised and ready for action.

If like me, you are addicted to counted embroidery, I hope this book will offer lots of stitching choices. If you are new to cross stitch – you have been warned – it may become an obsession!

Back to Basics

For some of you, this section will be repetition but it is useful to refresh your memory if you have not stitched for some time. Back to Basics clarifies the techniques needed for counted embroidery, particularly cross stitch and describes what materials and equipment you will need, how to use charts, how to prepare fabric and how to start stitching.

Basic Materials and Equipment

Fabrics

The fabrics used for counted embroidery are woven so that they have the same number of threads or blocks to 2.5cm (1in) in both directions. The warp and weft are woven evenly so when a stitch is formed it appears as a square or part of a square. When choosing fabrics for counted cross stitch, the thread count is the method used by manufacturers to differentiate between the varieties available, so the higher the number or the more threads or stitches to 2.5cm (1in), the finer the fabric.

Evenweaves, made from linen, cotton, acrylic, viscose, modal and mixtures of these, are woven singly and because single threads can be withdrawn, evenweaves are particularly suitable for withdrawn and pulled thread work. They are available in different colours, counts and bands. Zweigart have produced a

lovely antique-effect fabric called Vintage (see picture), which I've used for the hollyhock design on page 18. It is available in 32-count and 28-count linen and in some Aida counts.

Aida is a fabric designed for counted cross stitch and is woven in blocks rather than singly, which creates very obvious squares and so is ideal for the less experienced. Aida is available in 8, 11, 14, 16, 18 and 20 blocks to 2.5cm (1in) and in many colours.

Threads

The most commonly used thread for counted embroidery is stranded cotton (floss), often incorrectly referred to as embroidery silk. I have used stranded cotton for many of the projects but have added some space-dyed threads, metallic threads and beads for additional sparkle and interest.

Needles

Use blunt tapestry needles for counted cross stitch. The most common sizes used are 24 and 26 but the size depends on the fabric being used and personal preference. I always use a gold-plated needle, finding the nickel variety much less satisfactory. Gold-plated needles are also very helpful if you have a nickel allergy and certainly make forming French knots and bullion knots much easier. If you are attempting to stitch a project with a large number of fractional stitches on Aida fabric, you may find

Using this book

• Measurements are in metric with imperial conversions in brackets – work with one or the other.
• All the designs have been stitched predominantly with DMC stranded cotton (floss). Anchor equivalents have been given where possible (in brackets) but remember that these cannot always be a perfect match, so feel free to experiment.
• I have used colour charts with additional symbols so you can visualize the designs more easily but you may photocopy the charts to enlarge them for your own use.
• Within each project you will find technical explanations and diagrams as necessary. Refer to the Stitch Library (pages

102–112) for how to work the stitches. These are described alphabetically but refer to the Index if necessary. The Library contains some stitches not included in *The Cross Stitcher's Bible*.
• Each chapter has two main projects, with full instructions and chart, followed by one or two smaller, quick-to-work projects that use parts of the larger charts or have their own chart.
• There is an extensive Motif Library on pages 76–101, which you can use to select a wide variety of flower motifs. These will be particularly useful when working smaller projects as you can substitute one motif for another (see also Calculating Design Size opposite).

a sharp needle helpful as you will need to pierce the centre of a fabric square. Avoid leaving any needle in the fabric unless it is gold plated as it may leave marks. If you are not sure what size needle to choose, check as follows: push the needle through the fabric – it should pass through without enlarging the hole, but also without falling through too easily.

Scissors

Use dressmaker's shears for cutting fabric and a small, sharp pair of pointed scissors for cutting embroidery threads. I keep mine on a ribbon around my neck or attached to a magnet so that I know where they are!

Frames and Hoops

I work my cross stitch in a sewing movement, so prefer the fabric rolled in my hand and rarely work with a frame or embroidery hoop. If you must use a hoop, please use one large enough to hold the complete design as moving a hoop across your beautifully formed stitches is criminal! If I need a frame for a large project I use a padded upholstered frame (see Suppliers).

Basic Techniques

Preparing Fabric

Washing fabric If your fabric is rather stiff and starchy it is because it has too much dressing (starch-like finishing added to give extra body after weaving) so wash before use. Hand wash in lukewarm water and dry naturally. This is very useful if the fabric has a well-defined crease as these can be difficult, although not impossible, to remove afterwards. Press the fabric if necessary before you begin stitching and trim the selvage or any rough edges.

Preserving edges When working with linen or linen mixtures, sew a narrow hem around all raw edges to preserve the edges for hemstitching when the project is completed. If preferred, you can over-lock the fabric on a sewing machine. Do avoid using masking tape as the adhesive creeps and attracts grime.

Finding the fabric centre Work from the middle of the fabric and middle of the chart to ensure your design is centred on the fabric. Find the middle of the fabric by folding it in four and pressing lightly. On large projects, work a line of tacking (basting) threads to mark the folds, which should be removed when the project is completed. Tacking in and out of two threads or one Aida block will be useful when you are counting across the project later. Pressing the folds is sufficient on small pieces.

Working from Charts

The designs in this book are worked from charts and are counted designs. The charts are in colour with black and/or white symbols to aid colour identification and allow you to photocopy for your own use. Each square, both occupied and unoccupied, represents two threads of linen or one block of Aida and each occupied square equals one stitch unless stated otherwise.

When looking at a chart, try to plan your stitching direction. If you count across the shortest distances of empty fabric each time

you will avoid counting mistakes. To prevent serious errors, rule a line on the chart to match the centre using a colour pen.

You can turn your work and the chart upside down if you prefer to work towards you, but never turn halfway – your stitches will end up facing the wrong way! I make a copy of a chart so I can lightly colour it in as I proceed, to avoid looking at the wrong section. You may find a metal board with magnetic strips helpful as it keeps the chart in position and marks your place. With some projects it is useful to mark the top of the fabric in some way – I use a small safety pin so that I can tell immediately if the work is the wrong way up.

Calculating Design Size

The stitch count and finished design size are given with each project but being able to calculate the size of a finished design means that you will be able to work the designs on different fabric counts, to make them larger or smaller. You will also be able to work out how much fabric you need for a particular project or whether a design will fit a specific card or picture frame. Always add a generous margin when calculating fabric requirements, to allow for finishing and making up. I add 13cm (5in) to both dimensions when stitching a sampler.

Calculate design size as follows: count the number of stitches in each direction on the chart and then divide these numbers by the stitch count of your fabric.

For example, a design on 14-count Aida of 140 stitches x 140 stitches ÷ 14 = a design size of 10 x 10in (25 x 25cm).

When calculating design sizes for evenweave fabrics, divide the fabric count by 2 before you start, because evenweave is worked over two threads not one block as with Aida.

Starting and Finishing Stitching

Keep this process as simple and neat as you can and you will avoid problems later. I am not a fanatic and do not insist that the back is as neat as the front but if you keep the back tidy as you go, you will not have to spend an evening sorting it out later.

Knotless loop start This neat start can be used with an even number of strands i.e., 2, 4 or 6. To stitch with two strands, begin with one strand twice the length normally needed – about 80cm (30in). Double the thread and thread the needle with the two ends. Put the needle up through the fabric from the wrong side, where you intend to begin stitching, leaving the loop at the back of the work (see Fig 1). Form a half cross stitch, put the needle back through the fabric and through the waiting loop. The stitch is now anchored and you may begin.

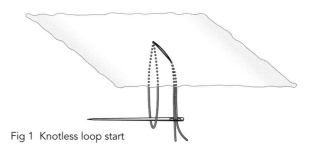

Fig 1 Knotless loop start

Away waste knot Start this way if using an odd number of strands, when tweeding, when using space-dyed threads or when you need a longer length of thread. Thread your needle with the number of strands required and knot the end. Insert the needle into the right side of the fabric away from where you wish to begin stitching (see Fig 2). Work your stitching towards the knot and cut it off when the threads are anchored. The alternative is to snip off the knot, thread a needle with the remaining length of thread and work under a few stitches to anchor it. If using a dark colour the knot may leave a shadow but this is easily removed with a clean toothbrush.

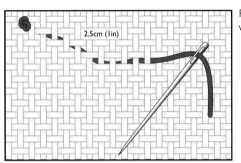

Fig 2 Away waste knot start

2.5cm (1in)

Finishing stitching At the back of the work, pass the needle and thread under several stitches of the same or similar colour, and then snip off the loose end close to the stitching. You can begin a new colour in a similar way.

Cross Stitching on Evenweave

An evenweave fabric may have thick and thin fibres and even quite dramatic slubs in the material. To even out any oddities in the weave, cross stitch is usually worked over *two threads* of an evenweave fabric.

An evenweave can also be worked over one thread, for miniature work or when fine detail is required (such as the bees on page 22). If working over one thread, each cross stitch must be completed rather than worked in two journeys because part of the stitch will tend to slip under the fabric threads. When working on evenweave over two fabric threads, start your first cross stitch to the left of a vertical thread (Fig 3). This makes it easier to spot counting mistakes because each stitch will start in the same position relevant to adjacent threads of the fabric.

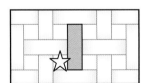

Fig 3 Starting to the left of a vertical thread

Cross stitches on evenweave can be formed individually (Fig 4) or in a sewing movement in two journeys, working half cross stitches along a row and then completing the cross stitches on the return journey (Fig 5). This is a quicker method, forming neat single vertical lines on the back, which give somewhere to finish off raw ends.

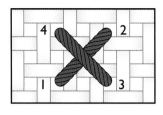

Fig 4 Single cross stitch on evenweave fabric

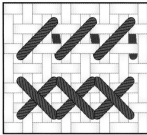

Fig 5 Cross stitch worked in two journeys on evenweave

Cross Stitching on Aida

When stitching on Aida, one block on the fabric corresponds to one square on a chart and generally cross stitch is worked over *one block*.

To work a cross stitch on Aida, refer to Fig 6, bringing the needle up from the wrong side of the fabric at the bottom left of a block. Cross one block diagonally and insert the needle into the top right corner. Come up at the bottom right corner and cross to the top left to complete the stitch. To work an adjacent stitch, bring the needle up at the bottom right corner of the first stitch. Cross stitches on Aida can be worked singly or in two journeys – work half cross stitches along a row and then complete the cross stitches on the return journey (as shown above for evenweave). Whichever way you choose, for a neat effect, make sure the top stitches all face in the same direction.

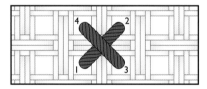

Fig 6 Single cross stitch on Aida fabric

Three-Quarter Cross Stitch

Three-quarter cross stitch is a fractional stitch that produces the illusion of curves. The stitch can be formed on either Aida or evenweave but is more successful on evenweave, as the formation of the cross stitch leaves a vacant hole for the fractional stitch.

Work the first half of the cross stitch as usual and then work the second 'quarter' stitch over the top and down into the central hole to anchor the first half of the stitch. If using Aida, push the needle through the centre of a block of the fabric.

Where two three-quarter stitches lie back to back in the space of a full cross stitch, work both of the respective 'quarter' stitches into the central hole.

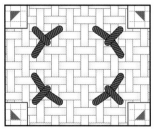

Fig 7 Three-quarter cross stitch on evenweave

Perfect Stitching

If you are a real cross stitch fanatic and examine your stitching through a magnifier, this section is for you!

• Organize your threads before you start a project as this will help to avoid problems later. Always include the manufacturer's name and shade number.

• Plan your route around the chart, counting over short distances to avoid mistakes. Remember to count fabric threads rather than holes and you will be less likely to make errors.

• Start stitching with an away waste knot rather than the loop method, so that you do not reverse the twist on the thread. I have never managed to see the difference with the naked eye so just how particular are you?

• Always start stitching to the left of a vertical thread (see Fig 3 opposite), because as counted thread embroidery is based on two or four threads, you should always be in this position and it helps to avoid counting mistakes.

• When stitching with more than one strand of stranded cotton (floss), separate each strand and then re-combine as this will help prevent the threads twisting as you stitch. This is particularly relevant when using space-dyed threads

• As you stitch you may find that the threads start to corkscrew slightly and spoil the stitches. Turn the work upside down and allow the needle to spin, or better still, each time you take the needle out of the fabric give it a half turn before you re-insert it and the stitches will lie flat.

• Try railroading: this term, originally used in the USA, refers to the technique used to force two strands of stranded cotton (floss) to lie flat and parallel to each other, which although time consuming does produce effective results. To railroad, pass the needle through the fabric between the two strands of stranded cotton (floss). You can select to railroad both parts of the cross stitch or only the top stitch. I find that half turning the needle (as described previously) can be as effective with less effort!

• Work your cross stitch in two directions in a sewing movement – half cross stitch in one direction and then cover those original stitches with the second row. This forms single vertical lines on the back that are very neat and give somewhere to finish raw ends.

• Remember that for neatest work the top stitches of each cross stitch should all face the same direction.

• Avoid coming up through occupied holes (where a stitch has already been formed) from the back. Instead, insert the needle from the front. This prevents spoiling existing stitches.

• If you are adding a backstitch outline, always add it after the cross stitch has been completed to prevent the solid line being broken. Work backstitches over each block, resisting the temptation to use longer stitches as this will show! You can use longer stitches to create flower stamens, cat's whiskers and so on.

Sensational
Spring Flowers

Spring is a time of optimism and thanks that the winter is over. It is a joy to see the bright green of young leaves on bare trees and the tips of bulbs peeping through the soil, promising a carpet of colour very soon. Every autumn I plant up lots of bowls and pots with spring bulbs, such as snowdrops, crocuses, daffodils, hyacinths, fritillaries, irises and tulips – then sit back and wait for the splash of colour, rather like the Hardanger Tulip Bowl opposite. This vibrant design is worked on checked linen, giving it a lovely rustic look. The design also features some beautiful Hardanger motifs and a bold zigzag hemstitched border. Spring flowers also appear on a sampler on page 13, with stylized sprigs in little rows. Some of these motifs are used again to decorate a needlecase and handmade card.

Hardanger
Tulip Bowl

I really hope you enjoy stitching this bold design. It's actually very versatile as you could omit the hemstitch and the Hardanger sections and frame just the cross stitched tulips in their bowl (which means you could work it on Aida fabric if you prefer). I stitched it on checked evenweave, with the Hardanger motifs and the hemstitch band placed in specific positions on the fabric, but you could use a plain linen instead.

Stitch count 158 x 126 (whole design)
Design size 32 x 25.5cm (12½ x 10in)

You will need

- 41 x 41cm (16 x 16in) checked 25-count linen (Zweigart Art No.7644)
- Tapestry needles sizes 24 and 22
- Stranded cotton (floss) as listed in the chart key
- Anchor Multicolour Pearl, shade 1349
- Polyester wadding (batting)
- Coloured backing fabric
- Picture frame

1 Fold the fabric in four and mark the folds with tacking (basting) stitches. Oversew or hem raw fabric edges to prevent fraying. Using a loop start (page 7), begin stitching from the centre of the fabric and chart (on pages 16–17).

2 Using a size 24 needle, work over two linen threads using two strands of stranded cotton (floss) for full and three-quarter cross stitches, remembering to keep the top stitch facing the same direction. Use one strand for backstitches, in the shades given on the chart. (Instructions continue overleaf.)

Hardanger Coaster
Stitch count 46 x 46 **Design size** 9 x 9cm (3½ x 3½in)

This charming coaster features a pretty cross stitch motif repeated around some Hardanger embroidery (see page 16) and is perfect way to practise your skills. It was stitched on 26-count unbleached linen, using two strands for cross stitch and one for backstitch. The Hardanger was worked in cream perlé 8 for Kloster blocks and cream perlé 12 for needleweaving. A border of four-sided stitch over four threads in perlé 8 and a little fraying completes the project.

3 To work the Hardanger: I have placed my Hardanger sections using the pattern on the fabric rather than counting to the position. Change to a size 22 needle and start by working the Kloster blocks (see Technique Focus below and page 107), using one strand of Multicolour Pearl thread, counting over four threads of the linen. Check that the stitches are formed correctly and that the horizontal and vertical blocks are directly opposite each other (see details below).

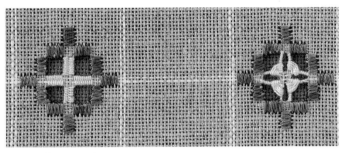

Needlewoven bars   Corner needleweaving with wrapped bars

Technique Focus

Hardanger Embroidery

At its simplest, Hardanger embroidery consists of three basic stages:
– stitching Kloster blocks
– cutting threads
– decorating the remaining threads and spaces.

✓ The secret of successful cutwork embroidery is working Kloster blocks accurately (the framework needed for the decorative filling stitches) and to count these blocks correctly (see diagram right). If they are in the *right* place the threads can be cut out and the stitching will *not* fall to pieces! See page 107 for full instructions on working Kloster blocks.

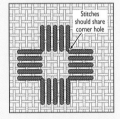

Stitches should share corner hole

✓ When all the Kloster blocks are complete and match everywhere, use sharp, pointed scissors to cut across the ends of the blocks, cutting only two threads at a time (see diagram left). The remaining threads and spaces can now be decorated.

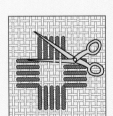

4 When all the blocks are completed and checked, cut the fabric threads – the red dotted lines on the chart indicate which threads to cut. Using sharp, pointed scissors, cut across the ends of the blocks slowly, counting and cutting two threads each time. When all the fabric threads are cut, remove the loose ends.

5 Add the filling stitches using one strand of cream (712) – I used needleweaving, corner needleweaving with wrapped bars and dove's eye stitches. Refer to the Stitch Library for working these stitches.

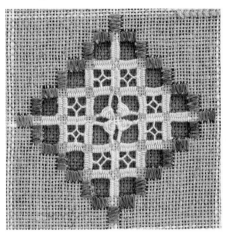

This stitching detail shows some corner needleweaving with wrapped bars (in the centre), surrounded by delicate dove's eye stitches and needlewoven bars

6 To work the hemstitch: Count out twelve fabric threads from the bottom left Hardanger motif and remove eight vertical fabric threads. Working in pairs, remove one thread completely and reweave the other into the gap (see page 106). Continue until all threads are removed or rewoven. Repeat the procedure across the bottom. You will be left with two fabric ladders joined at the corner with a square hole. Decorate the remaining threads with zigzag hemstitch (see page 112), and then work a spider's web (see page 110) in the corner hole, as shown below.

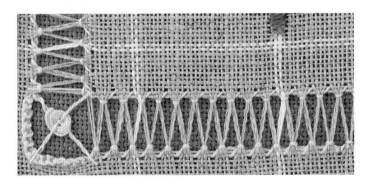

7 When stitching is complete, check for missed stitches, remove tacking (basting) and mount and frame as preferred. See page 113 for advice on framing and using wadding (batting) to enhance your embroidery. This project has the addition of some dark-coloured fabric under the embroidery to display the hemstitching and Hardanger to better effect.

Spring Flowers Sampler

This is a delicate little sampler (pictured on page 15). If preferred, you could stitch it on Aida and replace the queen stitches with three-quarter cross stitches. See the Stitch Library for working the stitches.

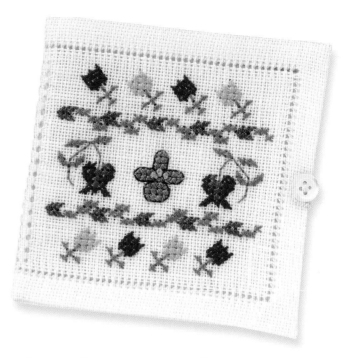

Stitch count 104 x 56
Design size 19 x 10cm (7½ x 4in)

You will need

• 33 x 23cm (13 x 9in) Cashel 28-count linen in lemon (Zweigart shade 227)
• Tapestry needle size 26
• Stranded cotton (floss) as listed in the chart key
• Polyester wadding (batting)
• Picture frame

1 Fold the fabric in four and mark the folds with tacking (basting) stitches. Oversew or hem raw fabric edges to prevent fraying. Using a loop start (page 7), begin stitching from the centre of the fabric and the chart overleaf.

2 Work over two linen threads (or one Aida block) using two strands of stranded cotton (floss) for full and three-quarter cross stitches and one strand for backstitches. Use two strands for French knots, queen stitches and braided cross stitches (seen in the detail above).

3 When all stitching is complete, remove tacking (basting) and then mount and frame. Refer to page 113 for advice on framing and using wadding (batting) to enhance your embroidery.

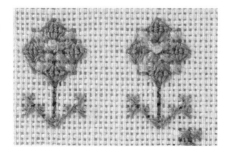

Tiny Flowers Needlecase

This delightful little case with a folded hem edge was stitched using motifs from the Spring Flowers Sampler chart overleaf. If preferred, you could replace this design with motifs from the Motif Library, perhaps combining a single motif with one of the little borders or frames charted on page 101.

Stitch count 33 x 34
Design size 6 x 6cm (2½ x 2½in)

You will need

• 20 x 14cm (8 x 5½in) Cashel 28-count ivory linen
• Mother-of-pearl button
• Piece of soft white flannel

1 Prepare your fabric for work. Fold it in half and work the design centred on the right-hand section.

2 Working over two threads of linen (or one Aida block), use two strands of stranded cotton (floss) for cross stitch and one for backstitch. Using two strands, work a line of four-sided stitch over four fabric threads to form the spine of the case. Work a folded hem around the edge of the front and back sections (instructions on page 106).

3 For the 'pages' of the needlecase, place a piece of folded flannel on the inside, slipstitching it to the wrong side of the four-sided stitches. To fasten the case, add a mother-of-pearl button and a button loop (see page 104).

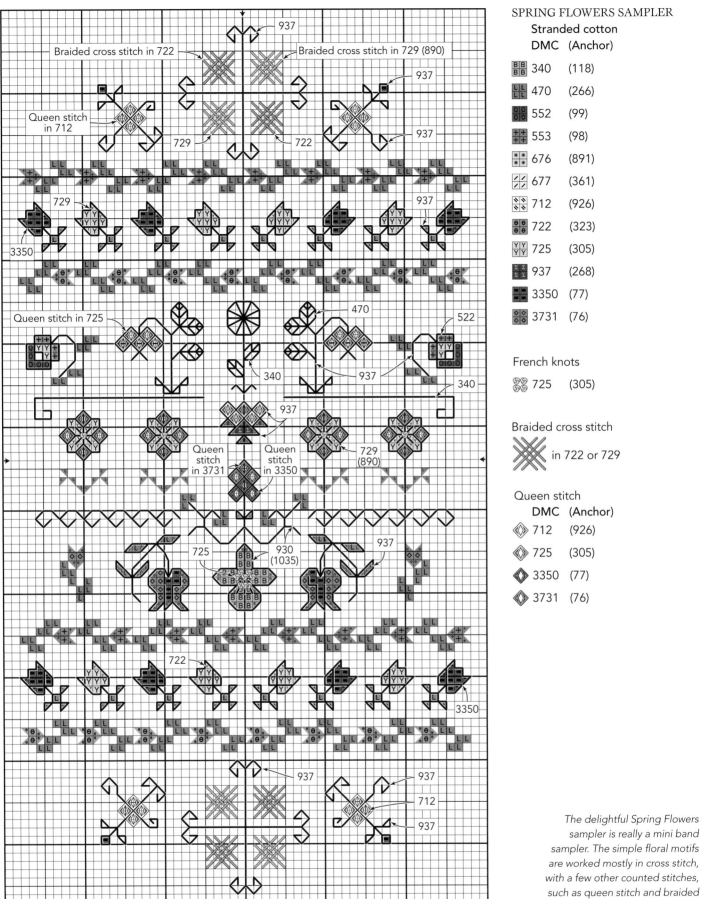

SPRING FLOWERS SAMPLER
Stranded cotton
DMC (Anchor)

B B / B B	340	(118)
L L / L L	470	(266)
◉◉ / ◉◉	552	(99)
+ + / + +	553	(98)
✳✳ / ✳✳	676	(891)
⁄⁄ / ⁄⁄	677	(361)
⣿⣿ / ⣿⣿	712	(926)
⊖⊖ / ⊖⊖	722	(323)
Y Y / Y Y	725	(305)
▨▨ / ▨▨	937	(268)
▦▦ / ▦▦	3350	(77)
◇◇ / ◇◇	3731	(76)

French knots

⣿⣿ 725 (305)

Braided cross stitch

✕✕✕ in 722 or 729

Queen stitch
DMC (Anchor)

◈	712	(926)
◈	725	(305)
◈	3350	(77)
◈	3731	(76)

The delightful Spring Flowers sampler is really a mini band sampler. The simple floral motifs are worked mostly in cross stitch, with a few other counted stitches, such as queen stitch and braided cross stitch, to add interest

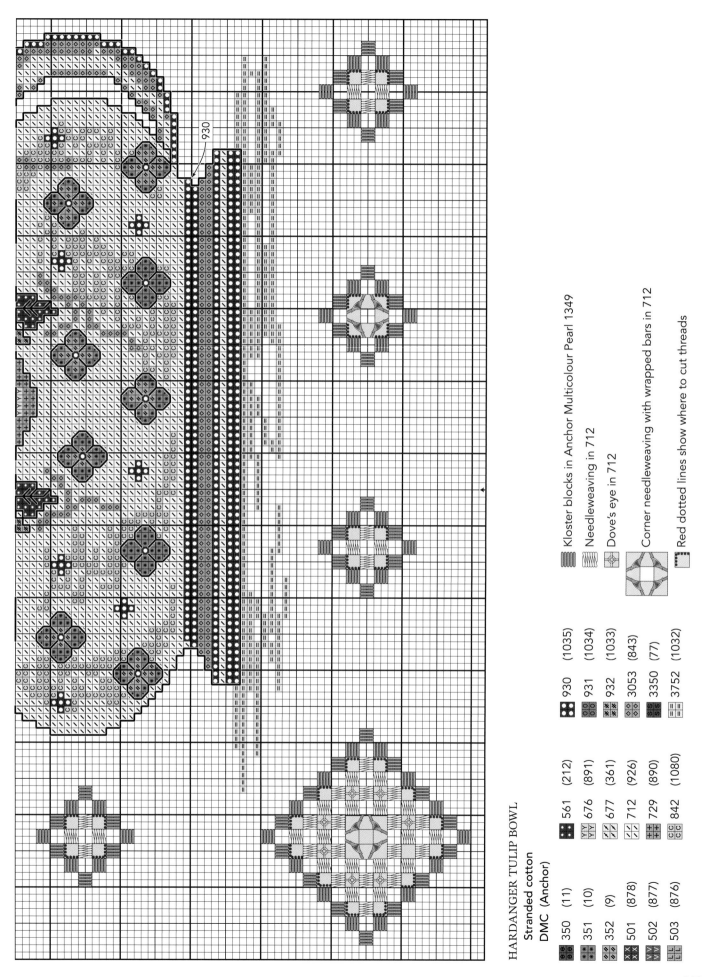

930

HARDANGER TULIP BOWL
Stranded cotton
DMC (Anchor)

350	(11)	561	(212)
351	(10)	676	(891)
352	(9)	677	(361)
501	(878)	712	(926)
502	(877)	729	(890)
503	(876)	842	(1080)

930	(1035)	
931	(1034)	
932	(1033)	
3053	(843)	
3350	(77)	
3752	(1032)	

Kloster blocks in Anchor Multicolour Pearl 1349

Needleweaving in 712

Dove's eye in 712

Corner needleweaving with wrapped bars in 712

Red dotted lines show where to cut threads

Cottage Garden Blooms

A thatched cottage surrounded by perennials and roses was the image that inpired me when I was designing this section of the book. I know these cottages exist but can only imagine how much work must be involved to create the chocolate-box gardens. They are such a glorious mass of flower – delphiniums, lupins, geraniums, phlox, lavender, foxglove and hollyhock, to name but a few. I've chosen the hollyhock as the main subject in this chapter because this gorgeous biennial flower reminds me of a visit to Claude Monet's garden at Giverny in France, where there are dozens of these towering plants in an enormous variety of colours. Another cottage-garden favourite is the stately foxglove, perfect to decorate a diary (overleaf). Bumblebees worked in fluffy velvet stitch also feature on a card (below).

Hollyhock and Bumblebees

For a dramatic cross stitch design I chose a hollyhock so deep in colour that it can look almost black in a certain light. On my version, pictured opposite, I have added two bumblebees stitched over just one fabric thread, which is only possible if you are working on evenweave fabric. If you want to use Aida fabric, you will need to work them over one block in the normal way, which means your bees will end up twice the size of mine!

Stitch count 150 x 74
Design size 27 x 13.5cm (10¾ x 5¼in)

You will need

- 40 x 25cm (16 x 10in) 28-count tea-dyed Vintage Cashel linen (Zweigart shade 3009)
- Tapestry needle size 26
- Stranded cotton (floss) as listed in the chart key
- Polyester wadding (batting)
- Picture frame

1 Fold the fabric in four and mark the folds with tacking (basting) stitches. Oversew or hem raw fabric edges to prevent fraying. Using a loop start (page 7), begin stitching from the centre of the fabric and chart (on pages 22–23).

2 Work the hollyhock cross stitch over two linen threads (or one Aida block) using two strands of stranded cotton (floss) for cross stitches and one strand for backstitches.

3 Work the bumblebees with one strand for cross stitch and backstitch over just one linen thread, working each cross stitch individually. When all cross stitch and backstitch is complete, add random French knots to the flower centre with two strands of yellow and then add slightly curly bullion knots (see the picture detail on page 23).

4 When stitching is complete, remove tacking (basting) and mount and frame as preferred. See page 113 for advice on framing and using wadding (batting) to enhance your embroidery.

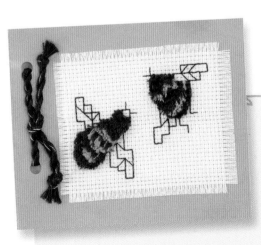

Fluffy Bumblebee Card
Stitch count 26 x 37   **Design size** 4.7 x 6.7cm (1¾ x 2½in)

Work these delightful bumblebees in the centre of a 10cm (4in) square of 14-count Star Aida. Use the chart on page 22 but work velvet stitch instead of cross stitch, using three strands of stranded cotton (floss). Add the backstitch in one strand of dark brown. Trim the velvet stitches with sharp scissors and fluff up with a soft brush. Make a simple gold card, trim the Aida to size, fray the edges and attach to the card with double-sided tape. Add a twisted cord as a trim (see page 118).

Foxglove Garden Diary

I like using my stitching and often make book or card patches rather than using purchased cards. This pretty diary is made very simply but still looks very effective. I have hemstitched the raw edge in matching green stranded cotton. If you are going to work your version on Aida, it is possible to work the hemstitch but without removing the fabric threads. If preferred, you could select your favourite flower from the Motif Library and stitch that instead. You could customize this design by using one of the alphabets in the Motif Library to add words or dates to the cross stitch design – see page 100 for advice.

Stitch count 93 x 39 (excluding hemstitch edge)
Design size 16.7 x 7cm (6½ x 2¾in)

You will need

- 30 x 20cm (12 x 8in) 28-count tea-dyed Vintage Cashel linen (Zweigart shade 3009)
- Stranded cotton (floss) as listed in the chart key
- Tapestry needle size 24
- Purchased notebook
- Double-sided tape

1 Fold the fabric in four and mark the folds with tacking (basting) stitches. Oversew or hem raw fabric edges to prevent fraying. Using a loop start (page 7), begin stitching from the centre of the fabric and chart opposite.

2 Work over two linen threads (or one Aida block) using two strands of stranded cotton (floss) for cross stitches and one for backstitches. Add French knots with two strands and two twists around the needle. If you wish, use two strands to backstitch the words 'My Garden Diary' or others of your choice in the space at the top right or bottom left, using an alphabet from page 100. If desired, you could embellish the design further by working on a larger piece of linen and adding a little floral border or frame all round using one of the designs charted on page 101.

3 When the stitching is complete, count out eight threads from the edge of the stitching and remove the ninth thread. Repeat on all four sides. Work a hemstitch edge (see page 106) using two strands of dark green stranded cotton (floss) and pulling firmly.

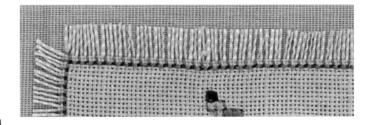

4 Trim away excess material and fray a narrow edge all round. To finish, mount the patch on to your book cover using double-sided tape.

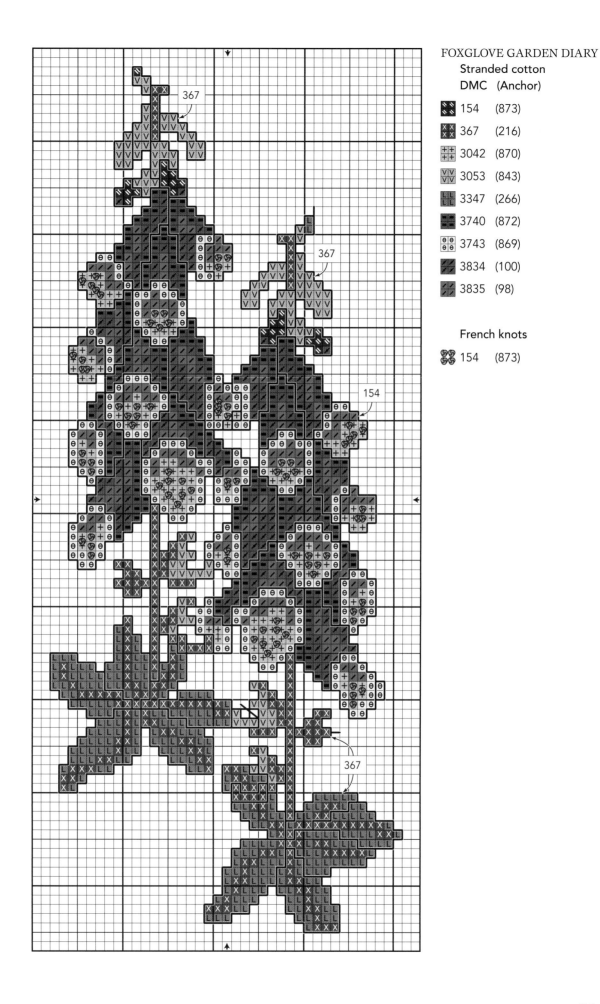

FOXGLOVE GARDEN DIARY

Stranded cotton

DMC (Anchor)

	DMC	(Anchor)
▧	154	(873)
X	367	(216)
+	3042	(870)
V	3053	(843)
L	3347	(266)
▦	3740	(872)
θ	3743	(869)
▨	3834	(100)
▧	3835	(98)

French knots

✿	154	(873)

Bumblebee motifs – cross stitch over 1 linen thread

898

937

902

902

HOLLYHOCK AND BUMBLEBEES

Stranded cotton

DMC (Anchor)

150	(59)	729	(890)	3347	(266)
520	(862)	777	(22)	3363	(262)
522	(860)	898	(380)	3685	(1028)
676	(891)	902	(897)	3831	(29)
725	(305)	937	(268)		

French knots

676 (891)

Bullion knots

676 (891)

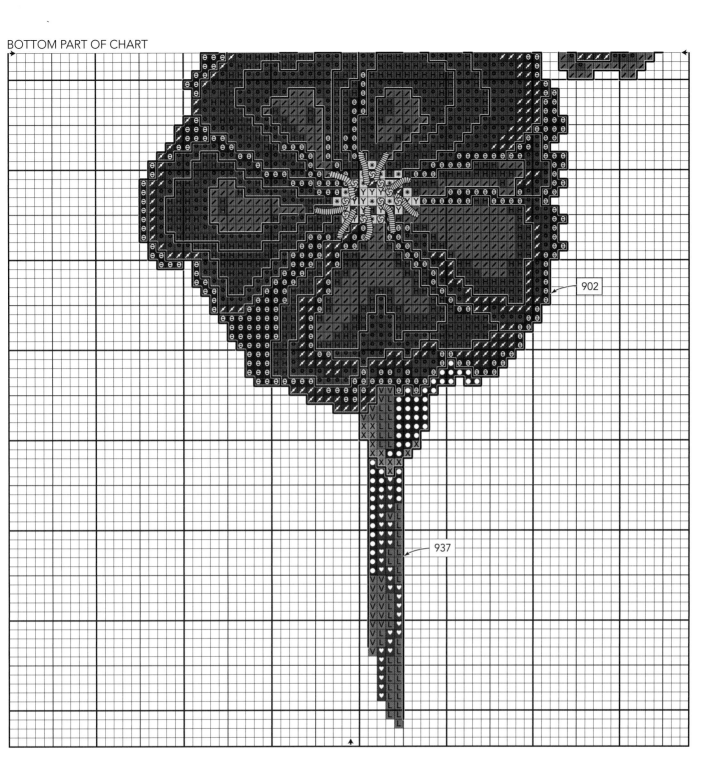

902

937

The French knots and curly bullion bars added to the centre of the hollyhock take a little extra time but are well worth the effort as they provide a glowing, contrasting colour in the centre of the flower, and also a three-dimensional quality, which adds to the realism of the design

Wonderful Wildflowers

I live in the country and plant wildflowers in parts of my garden in an attempt to produce a tiny meadow. This chapter was fairly hard to design because I simply did not know where to start. When I am out with my dogs, many of our walks are through fields of wildflowers, so how do you choose from so many delights?

I found some old engravings of meadow flowers and used these as inspiration for a Wildflower Stitch Sampler (top in picture opposite) and a Wildflower Charm Sampler (bottom). I've also stitched a harebell on a 'poppet' – my name for an unusual needle and scissor case (overleaf) and a poppy in a Hardanger heart (page 28).

Wildflower Stitch Sampler

This sampler is a real labour of love, with delicate spring flowers worked in cross stitch and decorative squares providing texture, and a challenge! If you prefer, you can omit these squares and work the design on Aida. To work it as shown you will need to use evenweave.

Stitch count 117 x 149
Design size 21 x 27cm (8½ x 10½in)

You will need

- 13 x 15in (33 x 38cm) antique white Zweigart Cashel 28-count linen
- Tapestry needle size 26
- Stranded cotton (floss) as listed in the chart key
- Polyester wadding (batting)
- Picture frame

1 Fold the fabric in four and mark the folds with tacking (basting) stitches. Oversew or hem raw fabric edges to prevent fraying. Using a loop start (page 7), begin stitching from the centre of the fabric and chart (on pages 30–31).

2 Work over two threads using two strands of stranded cotton (floss) for cross stitches and French knots and one strand for backstitches.

3 Refer to the Stitch Library for working all the different stitches in the squares. These are all worked in two strands, except the darning pattern (see detail, below left) which uses one strand. To work the pulled satin stitch in the middle square (see detail, below right), work with two strands of 712 and pull really firmly.

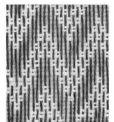 

4 When stitching is complete, remove tacking (basting) and mount and frame as preferred. See page 113 for framing and using wadding (batting).

Wildflower Chatelaine
Stitch count depends on motifs chosen

I wear a chatelaine whilst stitching to avoid the dangerous habit of putting needles in the arms of chairs or, worse, in my clothes! I have used motifs from the Wildflower Charm Sampler (chart on page 27) and the Poppy Hardanger Heart (chart on page 28) and omitted much of the backstitching for a simpler look. If preferred, you could select other flowers from the Motif Library. To make up, hem the two raw edges of the band, fold to the centre to form a point and slipstitch in place, adding a twisted cord (see page 118) to hold scissors. On the other end of the band I added a violet 'poppet' (see overleaf for instructions) to hold my thimble and so on.

Blue Harebell Poppet

I'm not sure if I invented this needle and scissor case but I am very pleased with it! The case is constructed over thin card and soft flannel with a twisted cord attached to the sliding section which holds needles. The harebell motif is charted on page 31 with a small detail on the back to match the one on the sliding section, which is pulled in and out of the Poppet with the twisted cord.

Stitch count 46 x 32 (for large harebell motif)
Design size 5 x 7.5cm (2 x 3in)

You will need

- One piece 10 x 7.5cm (4 x 3in) and two pieces 13 x 18cm (5 x 7in) of washed unbleached 35-count Zweigart Edinburgh linen (shade 52)
- Tapestry needle size 28
- Stranded cotton (floss) as listed in the chart key (but only 7 colours are used for the harebell)

1 Working from the centre of one of the larger pieces of linen, stitch the harebell motif from the chart on page 31, using one strand of stranded cotton (floss) over two fabric threads for cross stitches and backstitches. Work a small harebell on the other large piece of linen and another on the small linen piece.

2 When stitching is complete, press carefully and make up as described on page 117.

Wildflower Charm Sampler

Charms and a three-dimensional thistle add something extra to this design. Ensure that the charm is the correct size for the project. You could replace the flower motifs used in this sampler with others from the Motif Library.

Stitch count 94 x 98
Design size 18.5 x 19cm (7¼ x 7½in)

You will need

- 30 x 30cm (12 x 12in) ivory Zweigart Dublin 26-count linen
- Tapestry needle size 24
- Stranded cotton (floss) as listed in the chart key
- Three brass charms (bee, butterfly and dragonfly)
- Polyester wadding (batting)
- Picture frame

1 Fold the fabric in four and mark the folds with tacking (basting) stitches. Oversew or hem raw fabric edges to prevent fraying. Using a loop start (page 7), begin stitching from the centre of the fabric and chart opposite.

2 Work over two linen threads (or one Aida block) using two strands of stranded cotton (floss) for full and three-quarter cross stitches and French knots and one strand for backstitches.

3 To work the thistle flower, outline the base in one strand of thread and fill with random bullion knots with two strands. Work the top of the thistle in velvet stitch using two strands, trimming the stitched loops. Sew the charms on with matching thread.

4 When stitching is complete, remove tacking (basting) and mount and frame as preferred. See page 113 for advice on framing and using wadding (batting)

Technique Focus

Using Charms

Charms, buttons and other embellishments can transform the simplest cross stitch designs.

- ✓ Avoid cheap, stamped charms: they are made using strong processes and chemical residues may remain.
- ✓ Clean a charm thoroughly with paper towel before using it and if concerned, coat the back of the charm with clear nail varnish.
- ✓ Match the size and scale of the charms used with your cross stitch design.
- ✓ Attach charms with a loop start and thread that matches your fabric.

WILDFLOWER CHARM SAMPLER

Stranded cotton

DMC (Anchor)

						French knots
315 (1019)	470 (266)	502 (877)	553 (98)	729 (890)	3363 (262)	722 (323)
316 (1017)	471 (265)	503 (876)	554 (95)	744 (301)		725 (305)
340 (118)	472 (253)	550 (101)	722 (323)	745 (300)		729 (890)
341 (117)	501 (878)	552 (99)	725 (305)	937 (268)		

Poppy Hardanger Heart

One of the best-loved wildflowers is the poppy and in the picture opposite you can see how well this simple motif combines with some Hardanger embroidery worked in gorgeous variegated thread.

Stitch count 52 x 54
Design size 9.5 x 9.8cm (3¾ x 3⅞in)

You will need

• 23 x 23cm (9 x 9in) ivory 28-count Zweigart Cashel linen
• Tapestry needle sizes 24 and 22
• Stranded cotton (floss) as listed in the chart key
• Anchor Multicolour Pearl shade 1315
• Anchor Pearl No.12 in cream
• Wadding (batting)
• Picture frame

1 Fold the fabric in four and mark the folds with tacking (basting) stitches. Oversew or hem raw fabric edges to prevent fraying. Using a loop start (page 7) and a size 24 needle, begin stitching from the centre of the fabric and the chart below.

2 Work the poppy over two linen threads, using two strands of stranded cotton for full and three-quarter cross stitches and one strand for backstitches. Work French knots with two strands.

3 Change to a size 22 needle and using one strand of Anchor Multicolour Pearl thread, work the Kloster blocks as shown on the chart (see Technique Focus on page 12 and also page 107). When the Kloster blocks are complete, check that they are all in the correct place, and then cut the fabric threads (indicated by the red dotted lines on the chart). When removing these threads, take care not to remove threads from the poppy section. If disaster strikes, take a long thread from the edge of the fabric and reweave it into the space, trimming the ends as necessary. Remove any 'whiskers'. Using cream thread, decorate the remaining fabric threads as shown on the chart – see the Stitch Library for working needleweaving, dove's eye, corner dove's eye, spider's web and woven leaf.

4 When stitching is complete, remove tacking (basting) and mount and frame. See page 113 for advice on framing and using wadding (batting) to enhance your embroidery.

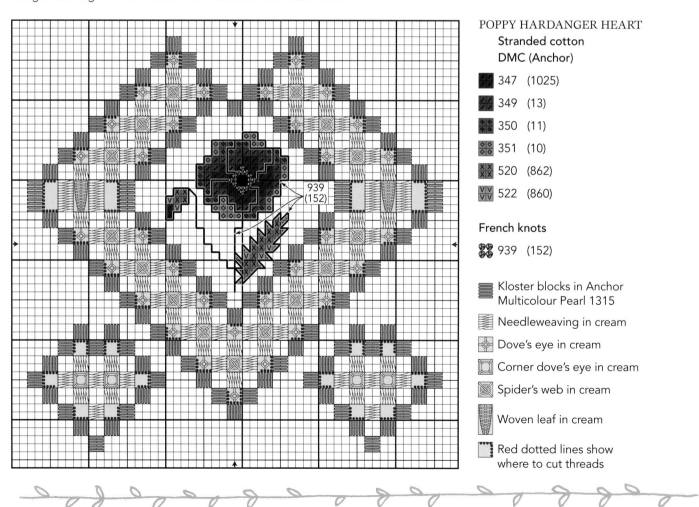

POPPY HARDANGER HEART

Stranded cotton
DMC (Anchor)

■	347	(1025)
◢	349	(13)
◣	350	(11)
◇	351	(10)
X	520	(862)
V	522	(860)

French knots

🕸 939 (152)

▤ Kloster blocks in Anchor Multicolour Pearl 1315

▥ Needleweaving in cream

✦ Dove's eye in cream

▣ Corner dove's eye in cream

▨ Spider's web in cream

▦ Woven leaf in cream

▢ Red dotted lines show where to cut threads

Long-legged cross stitch in 3838

Four-sided stitch in 712

930 (1035)

Rhodes stitch in 315

729

3838

930 (1035)

Double cross stitch in 3838

Algerian eye in 712

Diagonal satin stitch in 3838 and 725

729

550

3345 (268)

Vertical satin stitch in 712, 677, 3348, 470, 550, 553, 554

3838

Pulled satin stitch in 712

3838

Rhodes stitch in 729

Rice stitch in 729

3345 (268)

3347

930 (1035)

221

470

470

WILDFLOWER STITCH SAMPLER

Stranded cotton
DMC (Anchor)

221	(897)
223	(1027)
224	(895)
315	(1019)
316	(1017)
340	(118)
470	(266)
550	(101)
553	(98)
554	(95)
677	(361)
712	(926)
722	(324)
725	(305)
729	(890)
800	(144)
986	(246)
988	(243)
3347	(266)
3348	(264)
3838	(177)
3839	(176)

French knots

722 (324)

Labels within chart:
930 (1035)
Long-legged cross stitch in 729
Rhodes stitch in 315, 316
Satin stitch in 3347, 3838
3838
3838
Darning pattern (running stitch) in 316
Long-legged cross stitch in 223
986
315
3345 (268)
Half Rhodes stitch with a bar in 316

Romantic Roses

Roses have always been my favourite flower, both wild and cultivated. I don't know which I prefer, the overblown old-fashioned varieties with their wonderful heady scent or the wild briar roses seen in the hedgerows near my home. The designs in this section are inspired by images of roses in the famous book of prints, *Les Roses* by Pierre-Joseph Redouté. He was a French artist of the late 18th and early 19th century and his rose engravings are world famous and often used for cards, wrapping paper and gifts. We begin with a deep red rose, the ultimate symbol of romance, which I've worked as a picture but which could be stitched and made up in other ways, perhaps as a cushion for a romantic bedroom. I've also featured some pretty blackwork in this chapter for the Rosa Vulgaris overleaf.

Rich Red Rose

This gorgeous specimen rose is in rich reds and I hope that you can almost feel the velvety textures of the petals in the photograph opposite. The full-blown rose is worked on evenweave but, as you can see by the small rosebud gift card below, it could have been stitched on Aida fabric. Wadding (batting) was used behind the red rose embroidery to give it an attractive padded look.

Stitch count 194 x 115
Design size 37 x 21.5cm (14½ x 8½in)

You will need

- 53 x 40.5cm (21 x 16in) 27-count antique white Meran (Zweigart shade 100)
- Tapestry needle size 24
- Stranded cotton (floss) as listed in the chart key
- Polyester wadding (batting)
- Picture frame

1 Fold the fabric in four and mark the folds with tacking (basting) stitches. Oversew or hem the raw fabric edges to prevent fraying. Using a loop start (page 7), begin stitching from the centre of the fabric and chart on pages 36–37.

2 Work over two linen threads (or one block of Aida) using two strands of stranded cotton (floss) for the full and three-quarter cross stitches, remembering to keep the top stitch facing the same direction. Use one strand for backstitch, using the shades given on the chart. Resist the temptation to work the backstitch over more than one block or two threads or it will show through on the front!

3 When stitching is complete, check for missed stitches, remove tacking (basting) and mount and frame as preferred. See page 113 for advice on framing and using wadding (batting) to enhance your embroidery.

Rosebud Gift Card
Stitch count 65 x 18 **Design size** 12 x 3.25cm (4½ x 1¼in)

This pretty little card was made in an evening. I used the new Zweigart fabric called Star Aida, which has a frosted appearance without Lurex. Stitch the rosebud from the main chart on page 36, working over one block of 14-count and using two strands for cross stitch and one for backstitch. Fray the edges of the finished embroidery and use double-sided adhesive tape to stick it to your card. I made a black single-fold card embellished with red handmade paper and a glittery ribbon trim.

Rosa Vulgaris

This softly shaded rose has been worked twice, using two different counted stitching techniques to achieve very different effects – one in cross stitch and the other as a blackwork design. Both roses are worked on ivory evenweave but the cross stitch version could also be stitched on 14-count Aida. The blackwork rose could be worked on Aida but you may need a 'sharp' needle when working across part of a square.

Traditionally, blackwork is stitched by working the outline of a shape and filling the spaces with blackwork patterns, often in a combination of stranded cotton, silk and possibly metallics. I have charted this design using the same outline as the cross stitch version of the rose and filled it with various blackwork stitches in variegated threads. See page 98 for other blackwork patterns you could use.

Cross Stitch Rosa Vulgaris

Stitch count 83 x 64
Design size 16.2 x 12.5cm (6⅜ x 5in)

You will need

- 30.5 x 28cm (12 x 11in) 26-count ivory or antique white Zweigart Dublin linen
- Tapestry needle size 24
- Stranded cotton (floss) as listed in the chart key
- Polyester wadding (batting)
- Picture frame

1 Fold the fabric in four and mark the folds with tacking (basting) stitches and oversew or hem the raw fabric edges to prevent fraying. Beginning at the centre of the chart and fabric and using a loop start (page 7), follow the chart on page 38.

2 Work over two linen threads (or one Aida block) using two strands of stranded cotton (floss) for cross stitches, remembering to keep the top stitch facing the same direction. Add random French knots to the flower centre using two strands of DMC 352 (Anchor 1094). Use one strand for backstitches, in the shades given on the chart.

3 When stitching is complete, check for missed stitches, remove tacking (basting) and mount and frame as preferred. See page 113 for advice on framing and using wadding (batting) to enhance your embroidery.

Blackwork Rosa Vulgaris

Stitch count 80 x 64
Design size 14.5 x 12.5cm (5¾ x 5in)

You will need

- 30.5 x 28cm (12 x 11in) 28-count ivory or antique white Zweigart Dublin linen
- Tapestry needle size 24
- Stranded cotton (floss) as listed in the chart key
- Anchor Multicolour stranded cotton (floss), 1315 and 1355
- Madeira gold thread, No. 22
- Polyester wadding (batting)
- Picture frame

1 Fold the fabric in four and mark the folds with tacking (basting) stitches. Oversew or hem the raw fabric edges to prevent fraying. Beginning at the centre of the chart and fabric and using a loop start (page 7), follow the chart on page 39.

2 Work in Holbein stitch (see Technique Focus below) over two linen threads, beginning with the outlines of the rose, leaves and stems using two strands of black stranded cotton.

3 Using one strand of Anchor Multicolour thread in pinks, work the filling stitches for the flower face in Holbein stitch, adding gold thread as on the chart. Using one strand of Anchor Multicolour in greens, work the filling stitches for the leaves, adding the gold thread. See step 3, left, for finishing and framing your picture.

Technique Focus

Blackwork

You can bring a fresh look to a counted project by converting it into a charming blackwork design.

✓ Use the design outline as the pattern, working this in Holbein stitch (below) in a slightly thicker thread.

✓ Choose the blackwork patterns you want to work (or make up your own) and start to stitch from the centre of each shape, allowing the pattern to expand outwards to fill the void.

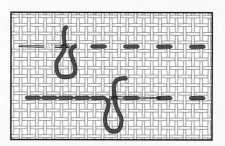

RICH RED ROSE

Stranded cotton
DMC (Anchor)

221 (1006)	783 (306)
321 (9046)	814 (44)
349 (335)	3051 (268)
350 (333)	3053 (264)
367 (245)	3046 (269)
676 (301)	3347 (239)
677 (386)	

3051

3051

3051

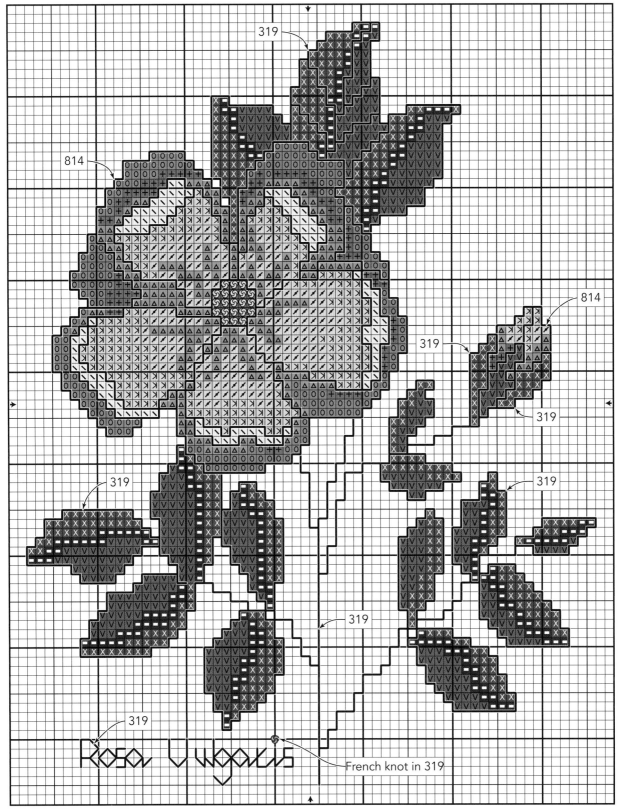

CROSS STITCH ROSA VULGARIS
   Stranded cotton
   DMC (Anchor)   French knots

   ▦ 319 (382)   ◩ 677 (386)   ▨ 725 (297)   ⊙ 3731 (54)   ✿ 319 (382)
   ✕✕ 367 (245)   ✚✚ 721 (333)   ■ 814 (44)   ✿ 352 (1094)
   ◪ 676 (301)   ▲▲ 722 (330)   ⱽⱽ 988 (227)

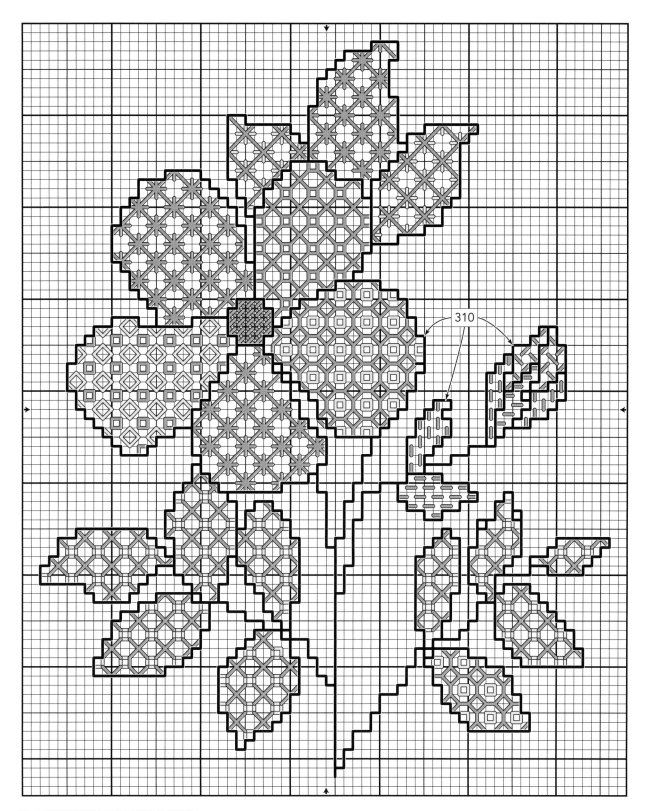

BLACKWORK ROSA VULGARIS

Anchor Multicolour
1315 for flowers

Anchor Multicolour
1355 for leaves
and buds

Madeira gold No.22

DMC 310 (Anchor 403)
backstitch outlines

DMC 725 (Anchor 297)
cross stitch in
flower centre

Lovely Lilies

Lilies can evoke strong emotions – some people love them and others dislike them as they are often the flower of choice at sad occasions. Lilies come in many different guises, from those that tower over our heads to dwarf patio types, but they are all so brilliant and vibrant in colour that they can only make you smile, and most have the most glorious fragrance. I have grown a variety of lilies in my garden and this year succeeded in rearing my own Stargazer lilies. I am quite sure that if I had tried to paint these beauties in their true colours, no one would have believed me. Nature is remarkable! In this chapter you can choose to work the impressive orange flame lilies picture, shown opposite, or smaller projects, such as the scissor case below or a series of pretty day lilies, overleaf.

Orange Flame Lilies

These flowers are a figment of my imagination but are, in truth, a mixture of a number of lily varieties. I have worked the picture on washed Dublin linen but the lily bouquet would also look lovely on coloured Aida, such as blue or black.

Stitch count 101 x 85
Design size 19.7 x 16.6cm (7¾ x 6½in)

You will need

- 33 x 30.5cm (13 x 12in) washed unbleached 26-count Dublin linen (Zweigart shade 52)
- Tapestry needle size 24
- Stranded cotton (floss) as listed in the chart key
- Anchor Marlitt rayon thread 1017 dark orange
- Polyester wadding (batting)
- Double coloured mount (mat)
- Picture frame

1 Fold the fabric in four and mark the folds with tacking (basting) stitches. Oversew or hem raw fabric edges to prevent fraying. Using a loop start (page 7), begin stitching from the centre of the fabric and chart on page 46.

2 Work over two linen threads (or one Aida block) using two strands of stranded cotton (floss) for cross stitches, remembering to keep the top stitch facing the same direction. Use one strand for backstitches and the long stitch stamens, in the shades given on the chart. Add the bullion knots (see page 103) in two strands of rayon thread.

3 When stitching is complete, check for missed stitches, remove tacking (basting) and mount and frame as preferred. See page 113 for advice on framing and using wadding (batting) to enhance your embroidery.

Yellow Lily Scissor Pad

Stitch count 30 x 27 (main lily motif only) **Design size** 5.4 x 5cm (2⅛ x 2in)
Finished pad size 13.5cm (5¼in) square approximately

This useful and unusual project has a secret: I have included a strong magnet in the polyester wadding (batting) inside the pad so that my scissors will stay put! I have stitched the design on evenweave so I could work the folded hem around the edge but it could be made up more simply in Aida. See page 47 for stitching and making up.

Day Lily Trio

This trio of lovely day lilies illustrate the versatility of a cross stitch chart. I have used the outline of a cross stitch day lily and worked two further versions in blackwork and darning patterns, to great effect I think. Each design is worked on a different fabric but all use stranded cottons (floss). The stitch count and design size is the same in each case. You could work all three designs on the same fabric rather than using a mount (mat), otherwise you will need a picture frame and a triple-aperture mount, as seen below.

Stitch count (for each lily) 58 x 43
Design size 10.5 x 7.8cm (4⅛ x 3in)

Cross Stitch Day Lily

The cross stitch version of the lily is very easy to stitch – perfect to decorate a bridal bag or other wedding accessory.

You will need

• 18 x 15cm (7 x 6in) cream 14-count Aida
• Tapestry needles sizes 24 and 26
• Stranded cotton (floss) as listed in the chart key

1 Fold the fabric in four and mark the folds with tacking (basting) stitches. Oversew or hem raw fabric edges to prevent fraying. Using a loop start (page 7), begin stitching from the centre of the fabric and chart.

2 Work over one Aida block, using two strands of stranded cotton (floss) for cross stitches and one for backstitches.

3 When stitching is complete, remove tacking (basting) and mount and frame as preferred. See page 113 for advice on framing and using wadding (batting).

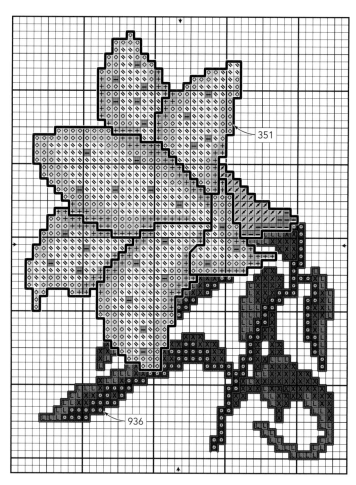

CROSS STITCH DAY LILY
Stranded cotton
DMC (Anchor)

351 (10)	712 (929)
352 (9)	761 (1021)
353 (8)	936 (846)
469 (267)	
470 (266)	

Blackwork Day Lily

True blackwork can be worked in any colour. Traditionally, the outline is worked first, with filling patterns starting in the centre of a given area and expanding to fill the space. Select other blackwork patterns (page 98) if you prefer.

You will need

- 18 x 15cm (7 x 6in) antique white Zweigart Cashel 28-count linen
- Tapestry needle size 26
- Stranded cotton (floss) as listed in the chart key
- Madeira No.15 gold metallic (shade 22)

1 Prepare and begin stitching as for the cross stitch day lily on the previous page, but use the chart below.

2 Count to the leaves and stems and, working over two fabric threads, use two strands of stranded cotton (floss) for cross stitches and one for backstitch leaf outlines. Work the outline of the flower in Holbein stitch in two strands of black. Work the blackwork patterns in one strand of cotton or gold metallic thread (see also Technique Focus on page 35).

3 When stitching is complete, remove tacking (basting) and mount and frame as preferred.

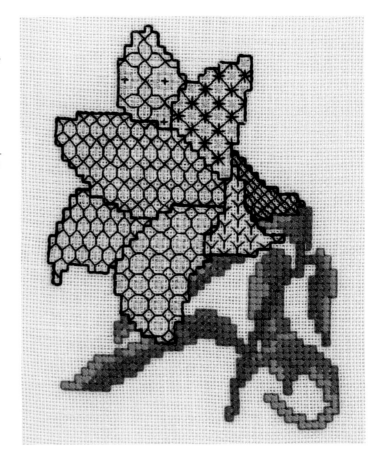

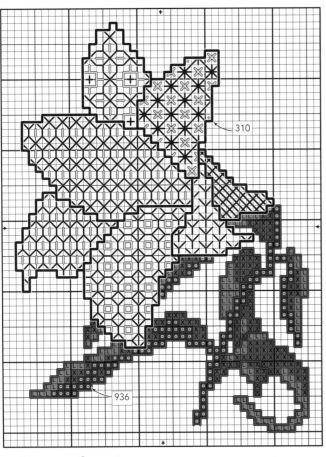

BLACKWORK DAY LILY
Stranded cotton
DMC (Anchor)

- 936 (846)
- 469 (267)
- 470 (266)
- 310 (403)
- Madeira No.15 gold metallic

Darning Day Lily

Darning patterns are very attractive and I have used a space-dyed thread for mine but you could create more complex projects using different colours (see page 99 for more patterns). Start the darning pattern in the centre of a designated area and allow the pattern to fill the space.

You will need

- 18 x 15cm (7 x 6in) ivory Zweigart Vintage Cashel 28-count linen (shade 1019)
- Tapestry needle size 26
- Stranded cotton (floss) as listed in the chart key
- Anchor Multicolour stranded cotton, shade 1315

1 Follow steps 1 and 2 of the cross stitch day lily on page 43 but use the chart below.

2 Counting carefully, work the outline of the lily flower in Holbein stitch (double running) or backstitch if preferred, using one strand of stranded cotton (floss). Add the pattern darning in one strand, working in running stitches throughout.

3 When stitching is complete, remove tacking (basting) and mount and frame as preferred.

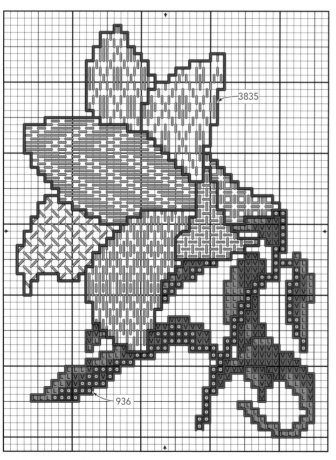

DARNING DAY LILY
Stranded cotton
DMC (Anchor)

936 (846)	
469 (267)	
470 (266)	
3835 (98)	
Pattern darning in Anchor Multicolour 1315	

937

3777 (1015)

3777 (1015)

3777 (1015)

Bullion knots
in Marlitt 1017

937

ORANGE FLAME LILIES
Stranded cotton
DMC (Anchor)

Bullion knots

					Bullion knots
349 (13)	722 (323)	743 (302)	937 (268)	3830 (5975)	Marlitt 1017
350 (11)	740 (316)	744 (301)	3346 (267)		
721 (324)	742 (303)	772 (259)	3347 (266)		

Yellow Lily Scissor Pad

This handy scissor pad (see picture on page 40) also doubles as a pincushion, and adding your initials using the charted alphabet below ensures that no-on will try to 'borrow' it! The folded and stitched hem is an attractive finishing touch. Many projects are beautifully finished off like this and it is invaluable for table linen. If desired, you could stitch other small motifs from the Motif Library.

You will need

- 20 x 20cm (8 x 8in) checked 28-count evenweave (Zweigart Art No.7644)
- Tapestry needle size 24
- Stranded cotton (floss) as listed in the chart key
- Anchor Marlitt rayon thread (822) yellow
- Polyester wadding (batting)
- Magnet (see Suppliers)

1 Fold the fabric in four and mark the folds with tacking (basting) stitches. Oversew or hem raw fabric edges to prevent fraying. Using a loop start (page 7), begin stitching the main lily motif from the centre of the fabric, using the chart below. If working motifs on patterned fabric, you will need to cut the fabric and place the motifs in the correct positions in relation to the fabric pattern.

2 Work over two linen threads (or one Aida block) using two strands of stranded cotton (floss) for cross stitches and one for backstitch. Work the small lily motifs within the linen checks and then stitch your initials. Using shiny yellow rayon thread, add the French knots and bullion knots to the lily stamens.

3 Check for missed stitches, remove tacking (basting) and stitch the folded hem following the instructions on page 106. Refer to page 118 for making up the pad.

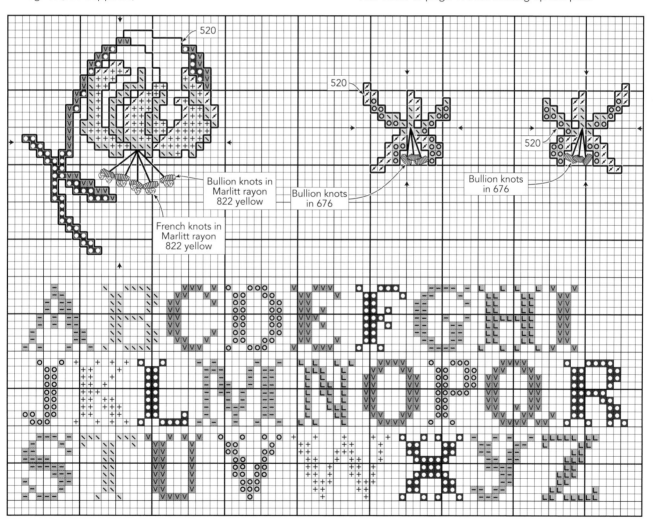

Bullion knots in Marlitt rayon 822 yellow

Bullion knots in 676

Bullion knots in 676

French knots in Marlitt rayon 822 yellow

YELLOW LILY SCISSOR PAD

Stranded cotton

DMC (Anchor)

676 (891)	712 (926)	522 (860)	
725 (305)	745 (300)	3364 (261)	
729 (890)	520 (862)		

French knots
Marlitt rayon 822 yellow

Bullion knots
Marlitt rayon 822 yellow

Oriental Orchids

The orchid house that I visited whilst on holiday in Sri Lanka a few years ago was an inspiration. I had no idea that orchids came in such a variety of colour and form and now have a couple of lovely plants in my conservatory. I have chosen two extremes as examples of these extraordinary flowers, the moth orchid (opposite) and the bumblebee orchid (overleaf), and have made them up as beautiful framed pictures. I've stitched a less rare variety as a little gift card (below) and worked a single flower for a trinket pot on page 52. All of these projects would work on black or dark blue fabric if you are prepared for the visual challenge!

Hot Pink Orchid

This orchid is commonly called a moth orchid because of the way it looks. The brightly coloured flower could be worked very effectively on a dark background, even on black. If you wish, you could add blending filament to the light colours to emulate the glisten that orchids have – see the Technique Focus on page 62 for advice on using blending filaments.

Stitch count 126 x 99
Design size 23 x 18cm (9 x 7in)

You will need

- 36 x 30cm (14 x 12in) pale green 28-count Zweigart Vintage Cashel linen
- Tapestry needle size 26
- Stranded cotton (floss) as listed in the chart key
- Polyester wadding (batting)
- Picture frame

1 Fold the fabric in four and mark the folds with tacking (basting) stitches. Oversew or hem raw fabric edges to prevent fraying. Using a loop start (page 7), begin stitching from the centre of the fabric and chart on page 53.

2 Work over two linen threads (or one Aida block) using two strands of stranded cotton (floss) for cross stitches and one for backstitches. Add the optional French knots in the flower centres using two strands, winding twice around the needle.

3 When stitching is complete, remove tacking (basting) and mount and frame as preferred. See page 113 for advice on framing and using wadding (batting) to enhance your embroidery.

Three Orchid Card
Stitch count 26 x 74   **Design size** 4.7 x 13.5cm (1⅞ x 5¼in)

This lovely little card with its sweet orchid faces, has been worked over one block of 14-count Star Aida, using two strands of stranded cotton (floss) for cross stitches and one strand for backstitches. Use the chart on page 52 (or the alternate colourway on the same page). When all the stitching is complete, trim away the excess fabric and fray the raw edge all round. Use double-sided tape to stick the embroidery to some lilac handmade paper and then on to a cream card.

Bumblebee Orchid

Many orchids are named for their shape or because they look like insects. I have created my own version of an orchid in my Bumblebee Orchid, pictured opposite, worked on evenweave and embellished with optional glass seed beads. This project could be stitched on Aida fabric and if preferred you could omit the beads and add bullion bars and French knots instead.

Stitch count 180 x 108
Design size 33 x 20cm (13 x 8in)

You will need
- 46 x 33cm (18 x 13in) soft beige 27-count Zweigart Perlleinen
- Tapestry needle size 24 and a beading needle
- Stranded cotton (floss) as listed in the chart key
- Mill Hill small bugle beads 72053 bronze (optional)
- Mill Hill glass seed beads 02044 chocolate brown (optional)
- Polyester wadding (batting)
- Picture frame

1 Fold the fabric in four and mark the folds with tacking (basting) stitches. Oversew or hem raw fabric edges to prevent fraying. Using a loop start (page 7), begin stitching from the centre of the fabric and chart (on pages 54–55).

2 Work over two linen threads (or one Aida block) using two strands of stranded cotton (floss) for cross stitches and one for backstitches and the long stitch stamens, in the shade codes given on the chart.

3 Add the bugle beads to the stamens using one strand of matching cotton. Add the glass seed beads in the flower centres. (See also Technique Focus below.)

4 When stitching is complete, check for missed stitches, remove tacking (basting) and mount and frame as preferred. See page 113 for advice on framing and using wadding (batting) to enhance your embroidery.

Beads
Working with beads is great fun and easy; because you are working with one colour thread you need not work blocks of colour as for cross stitch but just work across the pattern row by row.

✓ Check the size of the beads you plan to use with your fabric, because if the beads are too large the design will distort and the beads will crowd on top of each other. A rough guide is that most seed beads are perfect for 14-count fabric or canvas.

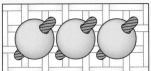

✓ Attach seed beads with a beading needle or a very fine 'sharp' needle using a half cross stitch and thread that matches the fabric background.
✓ Bugle beads make excellent flower stamens and, because they are longer than seed beads, are best attached after any cross stitch is completed.

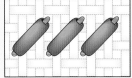

Seed beads and bugles make a lovely addition to this orchid design, the bronze and chocolate shades toning beautifully with the vibrant stranded cottons

Orchid Trinket Pot

I created a second peach colourway for the Three Orchid Card (charted below) and used one of the flowers to decorate this pretty trinket pot. I am sure you could create many more of your own and use them to make other items.

Stitch count 24 x 26
Design size 4.5 x 4.75cm (1¾ x 2in)

You will need

- 10 x 10cm (4 x 4in) 14-count Zweigart linen Aida
- Stranded cotton (floss) as listed in the chart key
- Tapestry needle size 24
- Polyester wadding (batting)
- Trinket pot (see Suppliers)

1 Fold the fabric in four and mark the folds with tacking (basting). Using a loop start (page 7), begin stitching from the centre of the fabric, following the chart below.

2 Work the cross stitch over one block of Aida (or two linen threads) using two strands of stranded cotton (floss) for the cross stitches, remembering to keep the top stitch facing the same direction. Use one strand for backstitch, in the shades on the chart.

3 When stitching is complete, remove tacking (basting) and mount in the pot lid according to the manufacturer's instructions, using the wadding for a padded look.

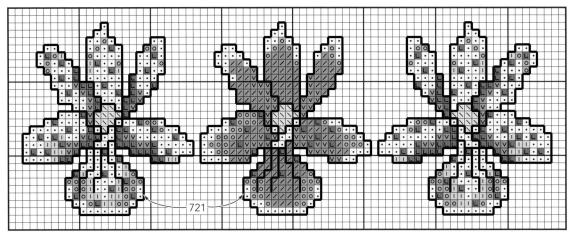

ALTERNATE PEACH COLOURWAY
Stranded cotton DMC (Anchor)

▨	351	(10)
◦◦	352	(9)
⊞	353	(8)
⊞	712	(926)
∟∟	721	(324)
∨∨	722	(323)
▨	725	(305)

THREE ORCHID CARD
Stranded cotton DMC (Anchor)

╱╱	153	(95)
▨	327	(101)
▨	550	(102)
╱╱	553	(98)
▨	554	(95)
◇◇	677	(361)
✱✱	725	(301)

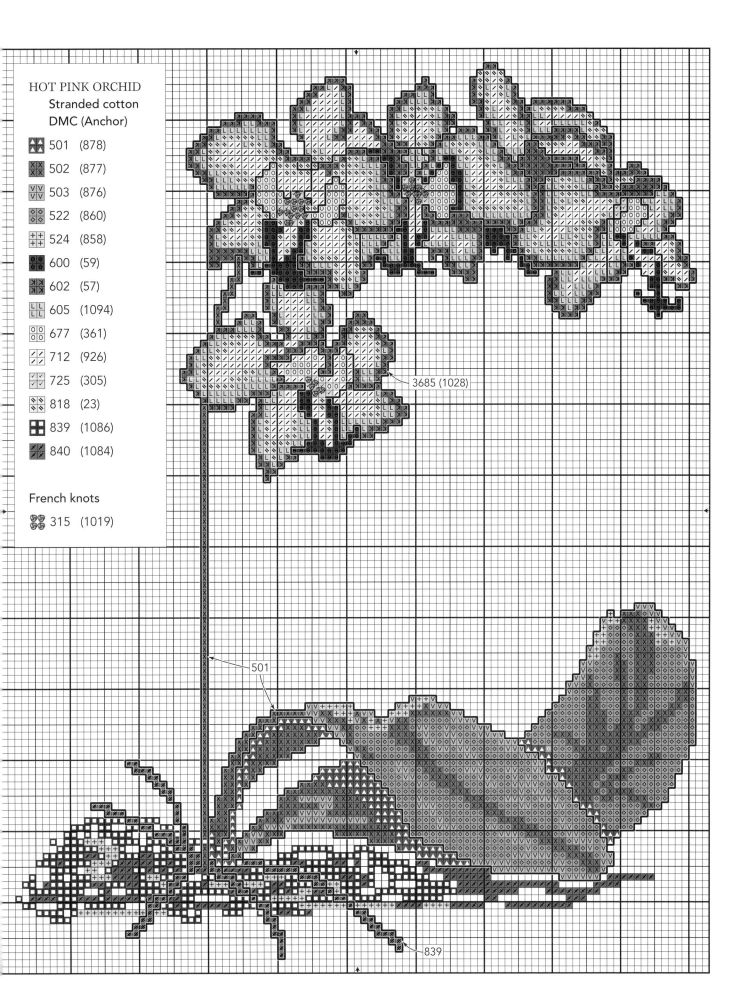

HOT PINK ORCHID
Stranded cotton
DMC (Anchor)

501 (878)
502 (877)
503 (876)
522 (860)
524 (858)
600 (59)
602 (57)
605 (1094)
677 (361)
712 (926)
725 (305)
818 (23)
839 (1086)
840 (1084)

French knots

315 (1019)

3685 (1028)

501

839

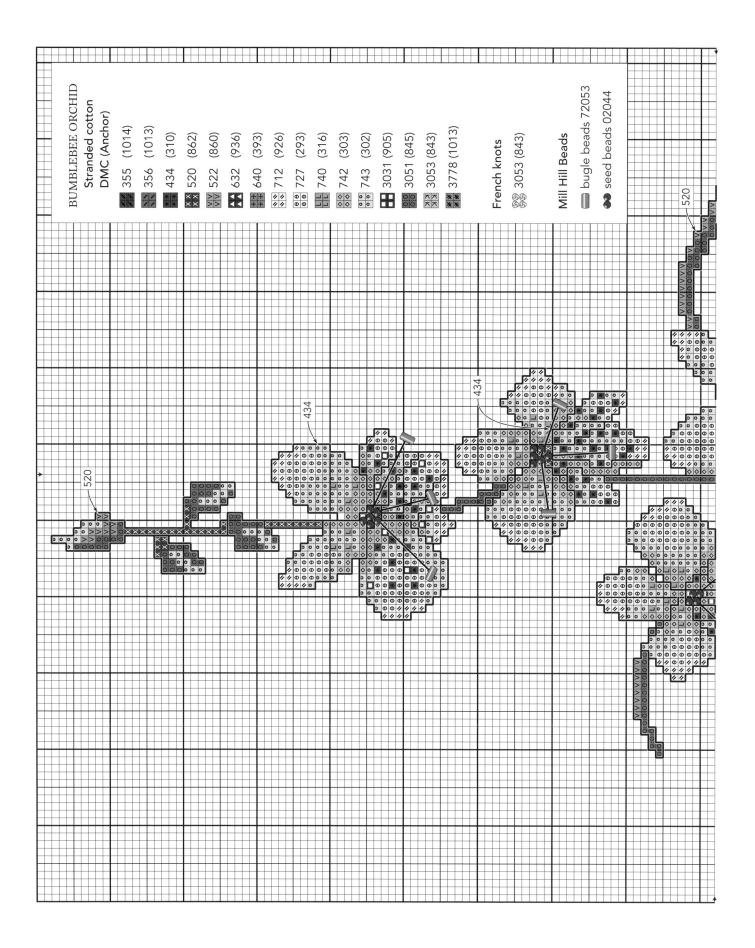

BUMBLEBEE ORCHID

Stranded cotton
DMC (Anchor)

355 (1014)
356 (1013)
434 (310)
520 (862)
522 (860)
632 (936)
640 (393)
712 (926)
727 (293)
740 (316)
742 (303)
743 (302)
3031 (905)
3051 (845)
3053 (843)
3778 (1013)

French knots
3053 (843)

Mill Hill Beads
bugle beads 72053
seed beads 02044

520

434

434

520

520

434

3031

3031

640

French knots in 3053

434

Extravagant Exotics

When our conservatory was built, I had hoped to have a mass of hibiscus and other exotic flowers hanging from the walls and ceiling but as it is, only very brave and long-suffering plants thrive on my neglect. I have been successful with amaryllis bulbs but only in their first season and before ravaged by my boisterous dogs! Undaunted, I have stitched these glorious flowers instead, as you can see opposite – a hummingbird and hibiscus picture and a beaded hibiscus cushion. There is also a beaded pincushion (below) and on page 58 an amaryllis inspired by a botanical print and given a lovely frosty gleam with blending filament.

Hummingbird and Hibiscus

This vibrant hibiscus is host to an exquisite hummingbird, using its long beak to collect nectar from the trumpet-shaped flowers. Adding blending filament to the threads for the bird will add a lifelike glisten (see also the Frosted Amaryllis, page 58). See page 62 for advice on using blending filaments. This design could also be stitched on 14-count Aida.

Stitch count 74 x 115
Design size 13.5 x 21cm (5¼ x 8¼in)

You will need
- 25.5 x 35.5cm (10 x 14in) 28-count ivory Zweigart Cashel linen
- Stranded cotton (floss) as listed in the chart key
- Mill Hill size 11 seed beads and 6mm bugle beads as listed in chart key
- Tapestry needle size 24 and a beading needle
- Polyester wadding (batting)
- Picture frame

1 Fold the fabric in four and mark the folds with tacking (basting) stitches, then oversew raw edges to prevent fraying. Beginning at the centre of the chart and fabric and using a loop start (page 7), follow the chart on page 60.

2 Work over two linen threads (or one Aida block) using two strands of stranded cotton (floss) for full and three-quarter cross stitches and one for backstitch, as given on the chart.

3 Add the seed beads on top of the cross stitches in the flower centre as shown below (see also Technique Focus, page 50). Work three long stitches and add peach bugle beads for the stamens, or replace bugles with bullion knots.

4 When stitching is complete remove tacking (basting) and mount and frame. See page 113 for advice on framing and using wadding (batting).

Beaded Hummingbird Pincushion
Stitch count 46 x 46   **Design size** 8.5 x 8.5cm (3¼ x 3¼in)

This sweet beaded hummingbird is simple to stitch on ivory 28-count Cashel linen using Mill Hill glass seed beads instead of stranded cotton (see chart on page 60 for the beads used). The beading was mounted into a wooden pincushion base (see Suppliers) and trimmed with a twisted cord (see page 118).

Beaded Hibiscus Cushion

You can stitch this wonderfully vibrant project (shown on the previous page) as pure cross stitch or highlight the flower centre and stamen with seed beads. Three strands of thread were used for the cross stitch to emphasize the strong colours against the bright fabric. I've inset the embroidery into a mitred cushion (pillow), but it could be framed as a picture instead. The design could also be worked on 14-count Aida.

Stitch count 86 x 96
Design size 16.2 x 18cm (6½ x 7in)

You will need

- 25.5 x 25.5cm (10 x 10in) 27-count yellow Meran evenweave (Zweigart shade 216)
- Tapestry needle size 24 and a beading needle
- Stranded cotton (floss) as listed in the chart key
- Mill Hill size 11 seed beads as listed in the chart key

1 Fold the fabric in four and mark the folds with tacking (basting) stitches and oversew raw edges to prevent fraying. Beginning at the centre of the chart and fabric and using a loop start (page 7), follow the chart on page 61.

2 Work over two linen threads (or one Aida block) using three strands of stranded cotton (floss) for cross stitches and one strand for backstitches as given on the chart.

3 Add the seed beads to the flower centre, stamen and down the leaf centres on top of the cross stitches, using the beads given in the key (see picture detail above and Technique Focus on page 50).

4 When stitching is complete, remove tacking (basting) and make up as a cushion, as described on page 116 or frame as a picture (page 113).

Frosted Amaryllis

This superb specimen (shown opposite) has been stitched on evenweave with pearl blending filament combined with the stranded cotton (floss) to create a frosted look. Blending filament is delicate but you will be amazed at the difference it makes to embroidery, adding a subtle gleam that catches the light beautifully. I have added bullion knots for the stamens but you could replace these with bugle beads. The design could also be worked on Aida.

Stitch count 179 x 104
Design size 33.6 x 19.5cm (13¼ x 7¾in)

You will need

- 51 x 35.5cm (20 x 14in) 27-count soft beige Perlleinen (Zweigart shade 53)
- Tapestry needle size 24
- Stranded cottons as listed in the chart key
- Kreinik blending filament, pearl 052F
- Polyester wadding (batting)
- Picture frame

1 Fold the fabric in four and mark folds with tacking (basting) stitches and oversew raw edges to prevent fraying. Beginning at the centre of the chart and fabric and using a loop start (page 7), follow the chart on pages 62–63, working over two linen threads (or one Aida block).

2 For the flower, use two strands of stranded cotton (floss) together with two strands of pearl blending filament for cross stitches. See Technique Focus page 62 for using blending filaments. Use one strand of stranded cotton for backstitch.

For the leaves, stem and pot, just use two strands of stranded cotton (floss) for the full and three-quarter cross stitches. Add the backstitch outlines in one strand in the shades on the chart.

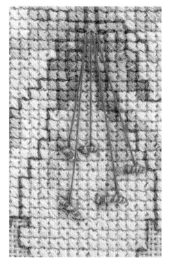

3 Work the long stitches for the stamens in one strand of dark peach, adding bullion knots (see page 103) in the postions shown on the chart.

4 When stitching is complete, remove tacking (basting), check for missed stitches and then mount and frame as preferred. See page 113 for advice on framing and using wadding (batting) to enhance your embroidery.

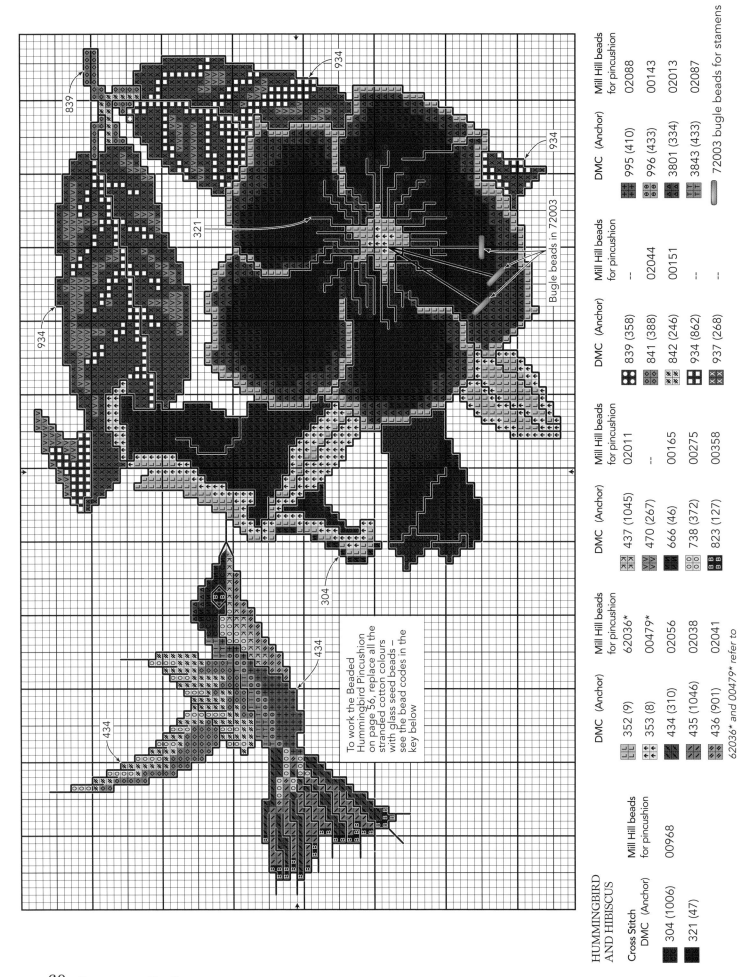

HUMMINGBIRD AND HIBISCUS

Cross Stitch

DMC	(Anchor)		Mill Hill beads for pincushion
304	(1006)		00968
321	(47)		

DMC	(Anchor)		Mill Hill beads for pincushion	DMC	(Anchor)		Mill Hill beads for pincushion	DMC	(Anchor)		Mill Hill beads for pincushion	DMC	(Anchor)		Mill Hill beads for pincushion
352	(9)		62036*	437	(1045)		02011	839	(358)		--	995	(410)		02088
353	(8)		00479*	470	(267)		--	841	(388)		02044	996	(433)		00143
434	(310)		02056	666	(46)		00165	842	(246)		00151	3801	(334)		02013
435	(1046)		02038	738	(372)		00275	934	(862)		--	3843	(433)		02087
436	(901)		02041	823	(127)		00358	937	(268)		--				

72003 bugle beads for stamens

62036* and 00479* refer to

To work the Beaded Hummingbird Pincushion on page 56, replace all the stranded cotton colours with glass seed beads – see the bead codes in the key below

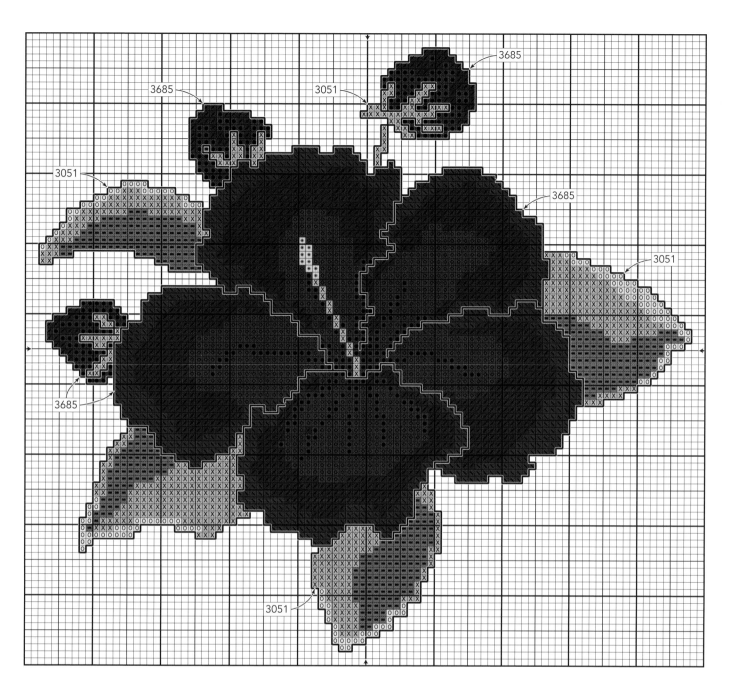

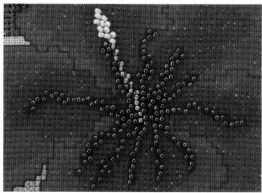

It is very easy to replace some of the cross stitch colours with seed beads and bring a lovely tactile quality to your work, as I have done here to highlight the centre of the hibiscus flower. Craft stores stock a wide range of bead colours for you to choose from.

BEADED HIBISCUS CUSHION
Stranded cotton

	DMC (Anchor)	Mill Hill Beads
▨	304 (1006)	--
◩	321 (47)	--
⊠	471 (265)	00167
⊡	472 (253)	--
■	666 (46)	02013
✳	725 (298)	00128
▦	3051 (681)	00332 (down leaf centre)
▩	3685 (69)	02012

Blending Filaments

Blending filaments can create some wonderful effects, especially with so many colours available today. You can vary the amount of shine by increasing or decreasing the number of strands you use.

✓ To thread blending filaments, fold the thread about 5cm (2in) from one end and insert the loop through the eye of the needle leaving a short tail. Pull the loop over the point of the needle and tighten the loop at the end of the eye to secure. Stroke the knot thread once to secure it in place.

✓ Stitch more slowly and attentively and use the 'stab' method rather than the 'hand sewing' method.

✓ Use short lengths of thread, 46cm (18in), to avoid excessive abrasion on the thread when pulling it through the fabric.

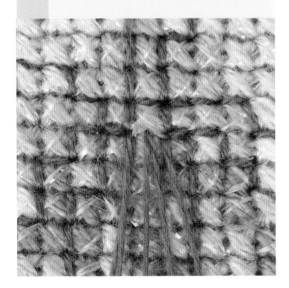

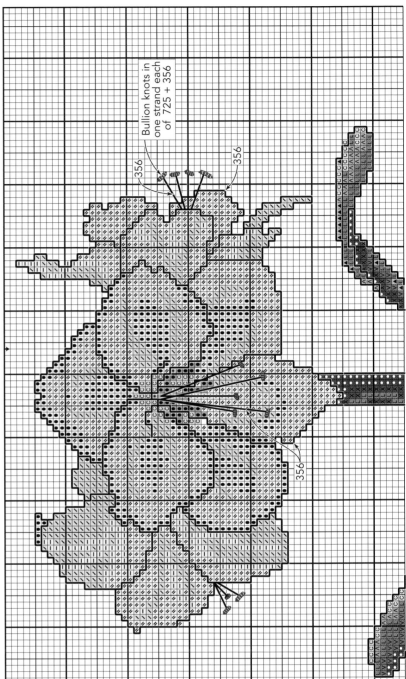

Bullion knots in one strand each of 725 + 356

356

356

356

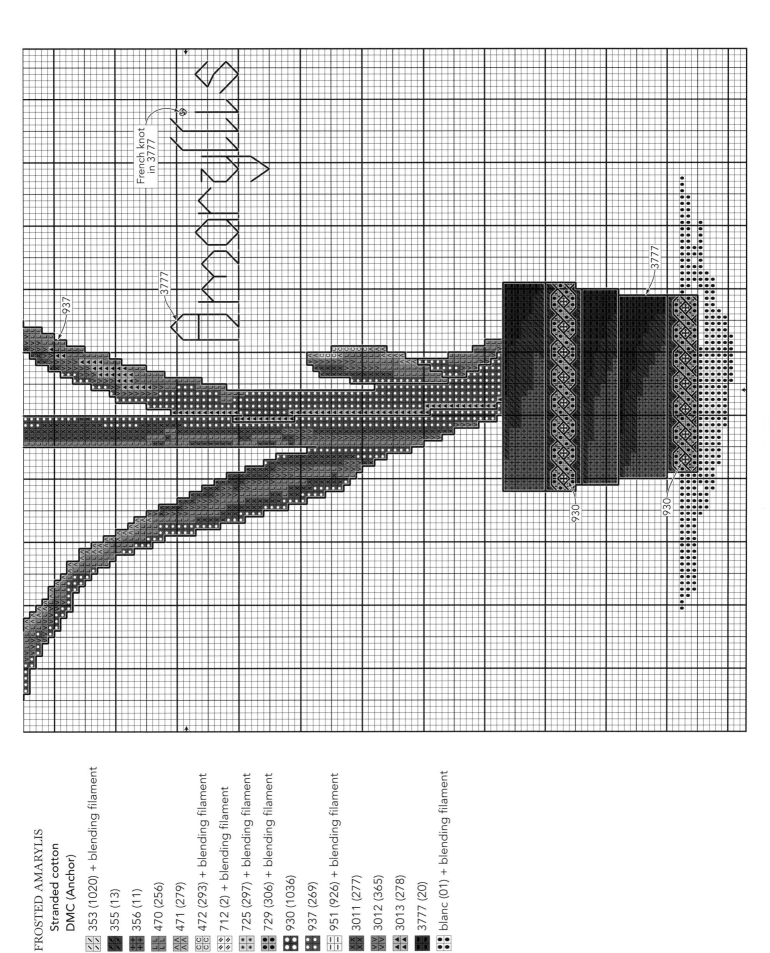

French knot in 3777

937

3777

3777

930

930

Amaryllis

FROSTED AMARYLLIS
Stranded cotton
DMC (Anchor)

- 353 (1020) + blending filament
- 355 (13)
- 356 (11)
- 470 (256)
- 471 (279)
- 472 (293) + blending filament
- 712 (2) + blending filament
- 725 (297) + blending filament
- 729 (306) + blending filament
- 930 (1036)
- 937 (269)
- 951 (926) + blending filament
- 3011 (277)
- 3012 (365)
- 3013 (278)
- 3777 (20)
- blanc (01) + blending filament

Colourful Climbers

Climbing plants abound both in the garden and in the conservatory. Some of these are seasonal and are only in their full glory in the summer, but others decorate the walls all year around. I find the colours of climbers very inspiring – whether it is the heavenly azure blue of morning glory, the scarlet of a passion flower or the dreamy shades of pink and lilac found in clematis. The colour range of clematis flowers in particular seems to get wider every year. There are so many gorgeous varieties to choose from. Some have small bell-shaped flowers, others sport huge star-like blooms, like the one I've used on my Clematis Trellis Cushion shown opposite. The enthusiastic passion flower also features in this chapter, adorning a purse with a lovely Hardanger edging (overleaf). There is also a morning glory design on page 68, which I've made up into a pretty glasses case.

Clematis Trellis Cushion

I love stitched cushions and have dozens in all shapes and sizes. This small cushion would look lovely with plain cushions. The trellis pattern suits the square shape very well and provides the perfect background for the vibrant clematis flowers. The flowers use only three colours so you could change the colourway, perhaps to soft lilac or pink.

Stitch count 116 x 101
Design size 21 x 18.5cm (8¼ x 7¼in)

You will need

- 33 x 30cm (13 x 12in) jade green 28-count Zweigart Jazlyn (shade 3626)
- Tapestry needle size 24
- Stranded cotton (floss) as listed in the chart key

1 Fold the fabric in four and mark the folds with tacking (basting) stitches. Oversew or hem raw fabric edges to prevent fraying. Using a loop start (page 7), begin stitching from the centre of the fabric and chart on page 69.

2 Work over two linen threads (or one Aida block) using two strands of stranded cotton (floss) for cross stitches, remembering to keep the top stitch facing the same direction. Use one strand for backstitches, in the shade codes given on the chart.

3 When stitching is complete, check for missed stitches, remove tacking (basting) and make up as a simple cushion, as described on page 115.

Beaded Clematis Amulet
Stitch count 46 x 50   **Design size** 8.5 x 9cm (3¼ x 3½in)

This clematis flower has been made up as a little neck purse. Use the top clematis from the chart on page 69 and work over one block of soft beige 14-count linen Aida, using two strands for cross stitches and one for backstitches. Using matching thread, add Mill Hill red seed beads (03003) in the flower centre and opalescent lilac (02024) seed beads along the veins in the petals. You could omit the beads if preferred. When the stitching is complete, make up as described on page 114.

Passion Flower Purse

Passion flowers are great climbers, quickly covering a wall or fence. This lovely purse is simpler to stitch and make up than it appears and is just stunning, especially with the added seed beads and bugle beads. The passion flowers glow with rich colours, while the Kloster blocks and buttonhole edging around the flap are worked in a bright variegated thread.

Stitch count 56 x 94 (front flap, including Hardanger and buttonhole edge)
Design size 9.5 x 16.5cm (3¾ x 6½in)
Finished size of purse 15 x 16cm (6 x 6½in) approx

You will need
- 55 x 26cm (22 x 10in) 28-count Cashel linen
- Tapestry needles sizes 24 and 22 and a beading needle
- Stranded cotton (floss) as listed in the chart key
- Anchor Multicolour Pearl No.8 in shade 1304
- Anchor Marlitt rayon 1017 dark orange
- Mill Hill glass seed beads 02011 opalescent flesh colour
- Mill Hill small bugle beads 72053 dusty pink

1 Fold the fabric in four and mark the folds with tacking (basting) stitches. Oversew or hem raw fabric edges to prevent fraying. Using a loop start (page 7), begin stitching from the centre of the fabric and chart opposite.

2 Work over two linen threads, using a size 24 needle and two strands of stranded cotton (floss) for cross stitches and one for backstitches. Add curly bullion knots at random in the flower centres using two strands of rayon thread.

3 To work the Hardanger on the front flap, change to a size 22 needle and work the Kloster blocks in one strand of Anchor Multicolour Pearl No.8, following the instructions on page 107. When these are complete check that they match correctly and then cut the fabric threads as indicated by the red dotted lines on the chart.

4 Sew on the beads using a beading needle and matching thread (see Technique Focus on page 50). Use one strand of Anchor Multicolour Pearl to work a border in buttonhole stitch (see page 103) over four threads, around the Hardanger section. When complete trim away excess fabric neatly.

5 When all stitching is complete, remove tacking (basting) and refer to page 116 for making up the purse.

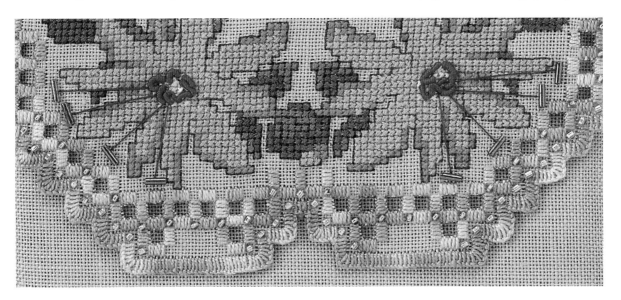

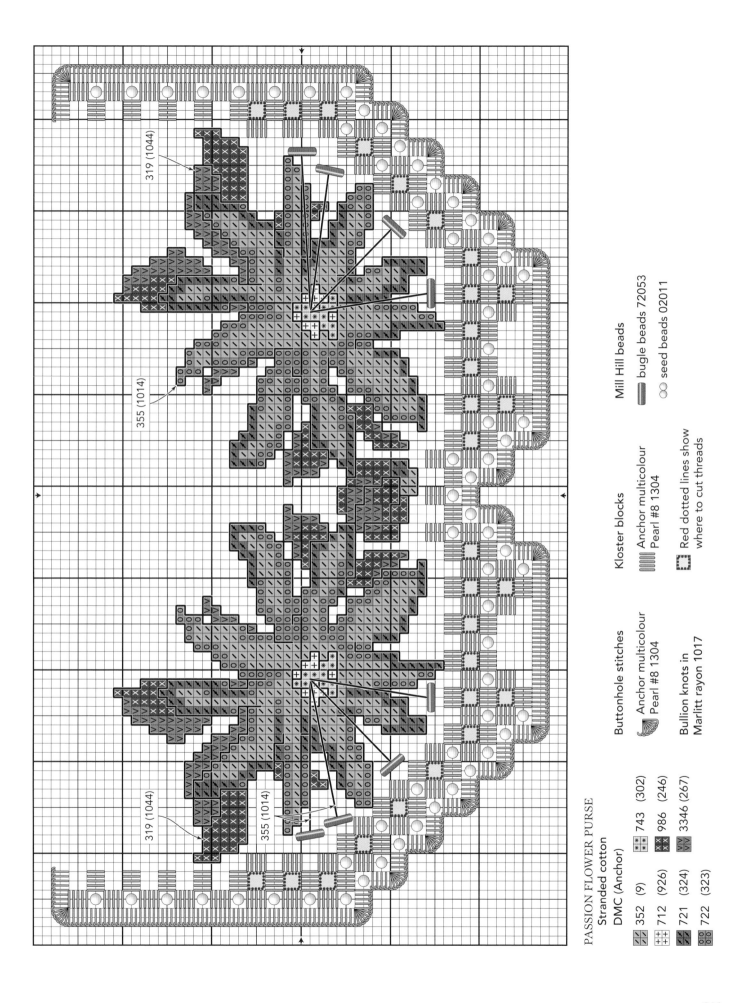

PASSION FLOWER PURSE
Stranded cotton
DMC (Anchor)

352 (9)
712 (926)
721 (324)
722 (323)
743 (302)
986 (246)
3346 (267)

319 (1044)
355 (1014)

Buttonhole stitches

Anchor multicolour
Pearl #8 1304

Bullion knots in
Marlitt rayon 1017

Kloster blocks

Anchor multicolour
Pearl #8 1304

Red dotted lines show
where to cut threads

Mill Hill beads

bugle beads 72053
seed beads 02011

Morning Glory Glasses Case

This pretty case features the lovely blue morning glory, which is the tender convolvulus variety that doesn't take over the garden forever! The case is simplicity itself to stitch and it could also be used for a mobile phone. There are many motifs in the Motif Library that you could stitch on the case instead of this design – what about a collection of little rosebuds framed by one of the borders on page 101?

Stitch count 105 x 48
Design size 14.8 x 6.7cm (5⅞ x 2¾in)

You will need

- 28 x 20cm (11 x 8in) cream 18-count Aida
- Tapestry needle size 24
- Stranded cotton (floss) as listed in the chart key

1 Prepare your fabric for work and then fold it in half. Using a loop start (page 7), begin stitching from the centre of the top half, using the chart here.

2 Work over one Aida block, using two strands of stranded cotton (floss) for cross stitches and one for backstitches in the shade codes given on the chart.

3 When stitching is complete, make up the case as described on page 115. The case has been edged with bias binding – you could buy some ready-made or make your own, as described on page 118.

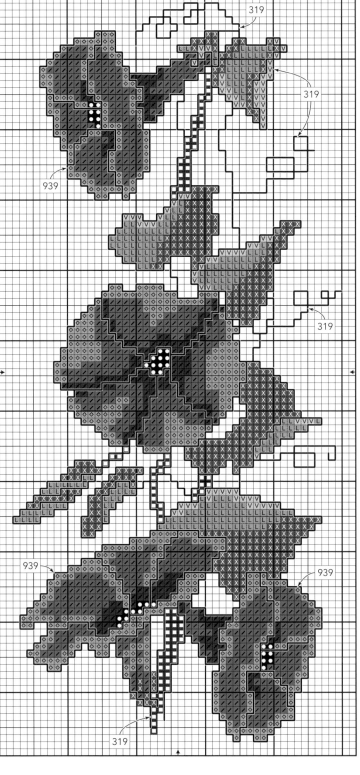

MORNING GLORY GLASSES CASE
Stranded cotton
DMC (Anchor)

⊞ 319 (1044)		◇◇ 799 (145)	
ᵛᵛ 368 (214)		⊞ 939 (152)	
▨ 797 (132)		ˣˣ 987 (244)	
▨ 798 (146)		ᴸᴸ 989 (242)	

CLEMATIS TRELLIS CUSHION
  Stranded cotton
  DMC (Anchor)

301 (1049)	470 (266)	722 (323)	841 (1080)	937 (268)	3687 (68)
434 (310)	471 (265)	839 (1086)	898 (380)	939 (152)	
436 (363)	712 (929)	840 (1084)	902 (897)	3685 (1028)	

Historical Flora

Flowers have appeared in counted embroidery from the earliest band samplers and spot samplers. Antique samplers feature flowers the stitcher would have known well – honeysuckle, pansy, rose and violet, to name but a few. This chapter was inspired by those delightful embroidered flowers and I think this might be one of my favourite sections as I am an avid collector of old embroideries and samplers. I had a lucky find one day when I spotted an old pole screen in a flea market and bought it for a song. It was the flowers in its Georgian frame that inspired the Antique Flowers Cushion pictured overleaf. The flower motifs used in the Jacobean Bell Pull, shown opposite, were taken from some line drawings in the Royal School of Needlework library, which I adapted for counted embroidery.

Jacobean Flower Bell Pull

This charming bell pull is an echo of the past, with its intertwining floral and insect motifs. Centuries ago, perfumed flowers were highly prized and what better flower to sweeten the air than honeysuckle or sweet woodbine. The wild pansy or heartsease was easily found in hedgerows, while carnations or gillyflowers had delicious clove-scented blooms.

Stitch count 187 x 62
Design size 34 x 11.3cm (13½ x 4½in)

You will need
- 46 x 23cm (18 x 9in) light stone 28-count Cashel linen (Zweigart shade 345)
- Tapestry needle size 26
- Stranded cotton (floss) as listed in the chart key

1 Fold the fabric in four and mark the folds with tacking (basting) stitches. Oversew or hem raw fabric edges to prevent fraying. Using a loop start (page 7), begin stitching from the centre of the fabric and chart (on pages 74–75).

2 Work over two linen threads (or one Aida block) using two strands of stranded cotton (floss) for cross stitches and one for backstitches. Using two strands add French knots to the honeysuckle and pansy flower centres and then add bullion knots around these French knots (see the enlarged detailed pictures with the chart). Outline the lower butterfly's body in backstitch and fill in with bullion knots.

3 When stitching is complete, check for missed stitches, remove tacking (basting) and make up as described on page 115.

Honeysuckle Notebook
Stitch count 80 x 45   **Design size** 15 x 9cm (6 x 3½in)

I have used some motifs from the Jacobean Flowers Bell Pull (chart on page 74) to create this pretty book insert. You could also apply the design as a patch. Stitch over one block of 14-count Zweigart Vintage Aida, using two strands of stranded cotton (floss) for cross stitches and one for backstitches. Add random French knots in lime green to the flower centre. I've omitted the couching from the honeysuckle. Use double-sided tape to fix the embroidery on the inside of your book cover aperture.

Antique Flowers Cushion

This design is reminiscent of the exuberant flower portraits by Dutch masters in the 17th century. I've made it up into a cushion with mitred corners but it would also look wonderful as a framed picture or a small wall hanging.

Stitch count 99 x 107
Design size 21 x 23cm (8¼ x 9in)

You will need

- 36 x 32cm (14 x 13in) washed unbleached 25-count Dublin linen (Zweigart shade 52)
- Tapestry needle size 24
- Stranded cotton (floss) as listed in the chart key

1 Fold the fabric in four and mark the folds with tacking (basting) stitches. Oversew or hem raw fabric edges to prevent fraying. Using a loop start (page 7), begin stitching from the centre of the fabric and chart opposite.

2 Work over two linen threads (or one Aida block) using two strands of stranded cotton (floss) for cross stitches and one for backstitches. Add the French knots and the bullion bars in two strands in the positions shown on the chart.

3 When stitching is complete, remove tacking (basting) and make up as a mitred cushion, as described on page 116.

ANTIQUE FLOWERS
CUSHION

Stranded cotton
DMC (Anchor)

315 (65)
316 (76)
347 (9046)
676 (891)
677 (386)
729 (306)
734 (279)
778 (103)
832 (307)
834 (278)
926 (850)
930 (1035)
931 (1034)
3011 (856)
3012 (855)
3013 (853)
3041 (871)
3042 (870)
3328 (1024)
3740 (872)
3743 (869)

French knots

676 (891)
725 (305)
3740 (872)

902 (897)

3011

902 (897)

930

French knots in 676 and 725

315

930

Bullion knots in 832, French knots in 3740

632 (936)

315

3011

Bullion knots in 832, French knots in 3740

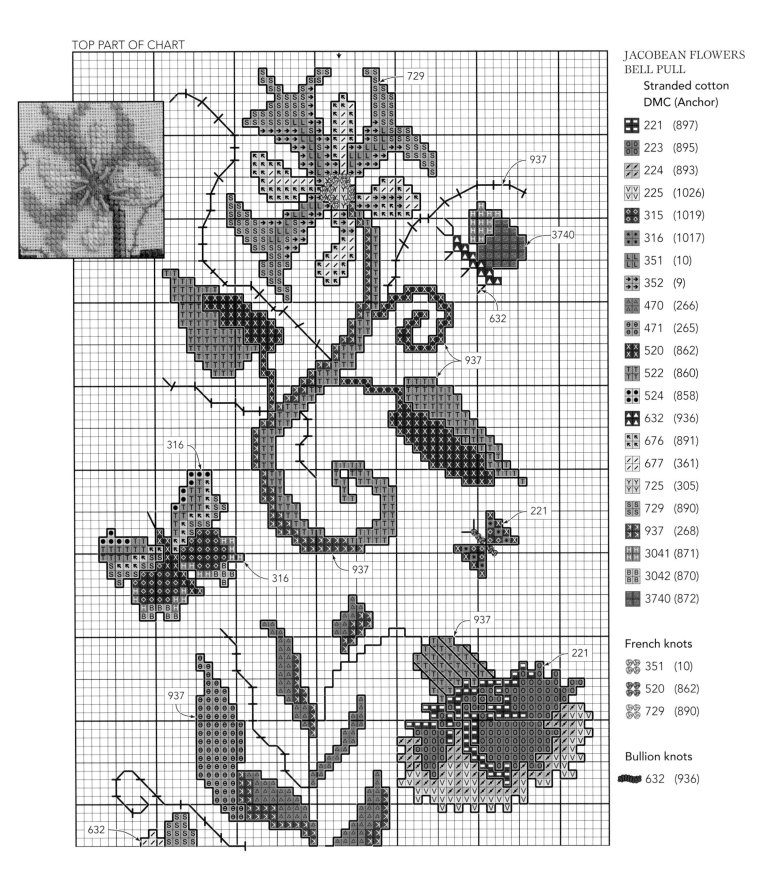

JACOBEAN FLOWERS
BELL PULL
Stranded cotton
DMC (Anchor)

⊞	221	(897)
🔲	223	(895)
⊘	224	(893)
⋁	225	(1026)
◈	315	(1019)
✳	316	(1017)
L	351	(10)
→	352	(9)
△	470	(266)
θ	471	(265)
X	520	(862)
T	522	(860)
⦂	524	(858)
▲	632	(936)
R	676	(891)
⁄	677	(361)
Y	725	(305)
S	729	(890)
⋈	937	(268)
H	3041	(871)
B	3042	(870)
▦	3740	(872)

French knots

🪢	351	(10)
🪢	520	(862)
🪢	729	(890)

Bullion knots

〰	632	(936)

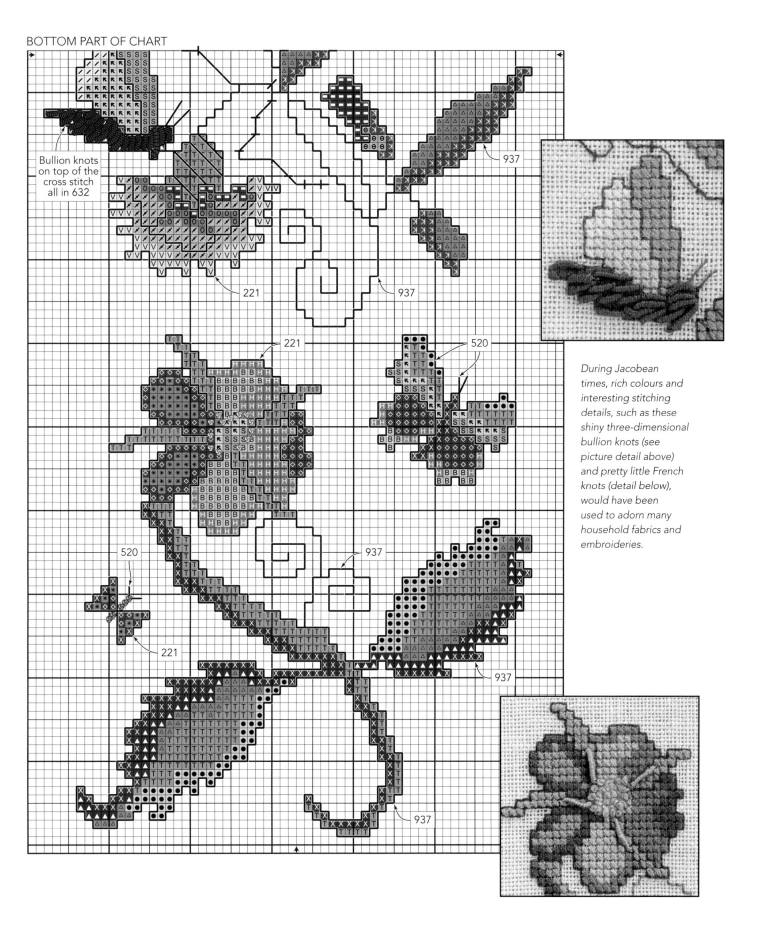

Bullion knots
on top of the
cross stitch
all in 632

937

221

221

520

520

221

937

937

937

*During Jacobean
times, rich colours and
interesting stitching
details, such as these
shiny three-dimensional
bullion knots (see
picture detail above)
and pretty little French
knots (detail below),
would have been
used to adorn many
household fabrics and
embroideries.*

Motif Library

I have designed 126 pretty flower motifs in this section for you to use in conjunction with or instead of the patterns in the book. I have created two pages of numbered cross stitch motifs for each flower group and I hope this will keep you occupied for hours! There is a colour key relating to each section and I have suggested outline colours and shades for French knots and so on. At the end of the library are further pages of blackwork and darning patterns, plus a selection of alphabets, numbers and little borders for you to use to customize the designs in this book.

As always, the idea of a Motif Library is that you select the motif you wish to use and then work it in your own way, so feel free to alter colours, combine patterns and mix and match as much as you like. I have worked a spot sampler here and have played around with the motifs a little, altering the colours in places as the fancy took me – a most relaxing and enjoyable way to stitch!

Overleaf you will see that I have worked a few of the motifs and made them into cards, sachets, trinket pots and book patches, but really the only limit is your own imagination. Many of the patterns can be worked on Aida or evenweave and any motif without fractional stitches can be worked on stitching paper.

Motif Projects

The small projects here will give you some ideas on how to use the Motif Library. I created the cards using handmade paper, ribbon, thin card and double-sided tape but you could use ready-made cards. The number with each project refers to the specific motif within the library.

Lily Pincushion (59)
Stitch count 35 x 35
Design size 7 x 7cm (2¾ x 2¾in)
This lily was stitched on cream 26-count Dublin linen and mounted in a wooden pincushion base (see Suppliers), using two strands of stranded cotton (floss) for cross stitch and one for backstitch.

Briar Rose Card (53)
Stitch count 29 x 22
Design size 4 x 5cm (1½ x 2in)
I stitched this card on 14-count Vintage Aida, with two strands of stranded cotton (floss) for cross stitch and one for backstitch. The card was completed using a circular card mount, handmade paper and opalescent ribbon.

Lily Card (61)
Stitch count 28 x 36
Design size 6.5 x 5cm (2½ x 2in)
This bright red lily, mounted on red corrugated card with a silver bow, was stitched on 14-count Lurex Aida using two strands of stranded cotton (floss) for cross stitch and one for backstitch. Add the stamens using one strand for the long stitches and two strands for the bullion knots.

Orchid Card (81)
Stitch count 40 x 30
Design size 6 x 8cm (2½ x 3in)
This unusual motif is worked on 26-count Dublin linen over two fabric threads and then the edges frayed as a simple patch. Use two strands of stranded cotton (floss) for cross stitch and one for backstitch. The card was completed using decorative papers and chiffon ribbon.

Vine Heart Box (110)
Stitch count 19 x 18
Design size 3.3 x 3.5cm (1¼ x 1⅜in)
I worked this motif on cream 14-count Aida using two strands of stranded cotton (floss) for cross stitch and one for backstitch. The design was mounted into a purchased cardboard box, which could be painted if preferred.

A flowerless room is a soulless room, to my way of thinking:
but even one solitary little vase of a living flower may redeem it.

(Vita Sackville-West)

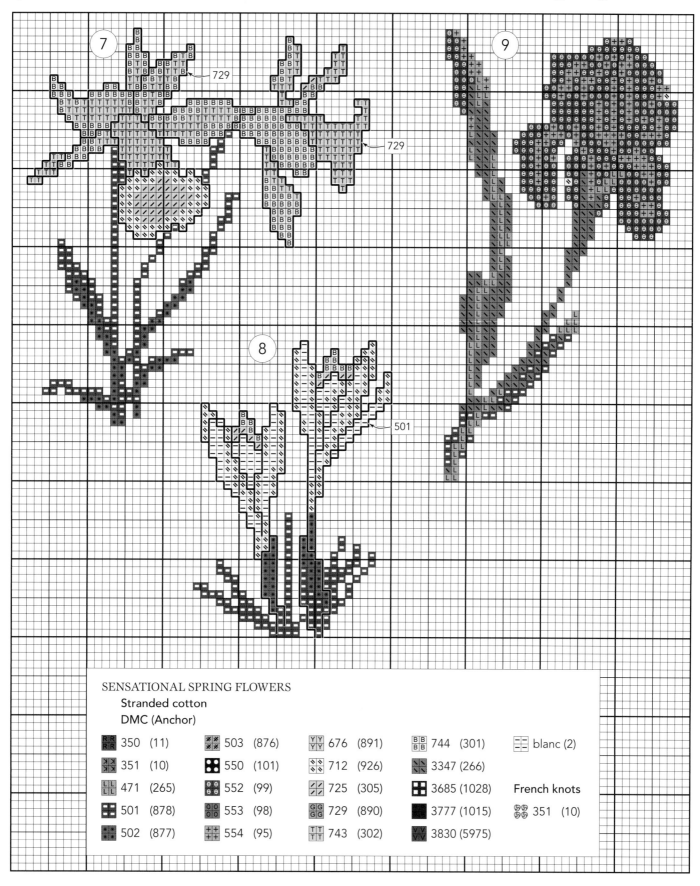

SENSATIONAL SPRING FLOWERS
Stranded cotton
DMC (Anchor)

350 (11)	503 (876)	676 (891)	744 (301)	blanc (2)
351 (10)	550 (101)	712 (926)	3347 (266)	
471 (265)	552 (99)	725 (305)	3685 (1028)	French knots
501 (878)	553 (98)	729 (890)	3777 (1015)	351 (10)
502 (877)	554 (95)	743 (302)	3830 (5975)	

*If I had but two loaves of bread, I would sell one and buy hyacinths,
for they would feed my soul.*
(Sheikh Muslih-vddin Saadi Shirazi)

Cottage Garden Blooms

There's rosemary, that's for remembrance; pray you, love, remember.
And there is pansies, that's for thoughts.

(William Shakespeare)

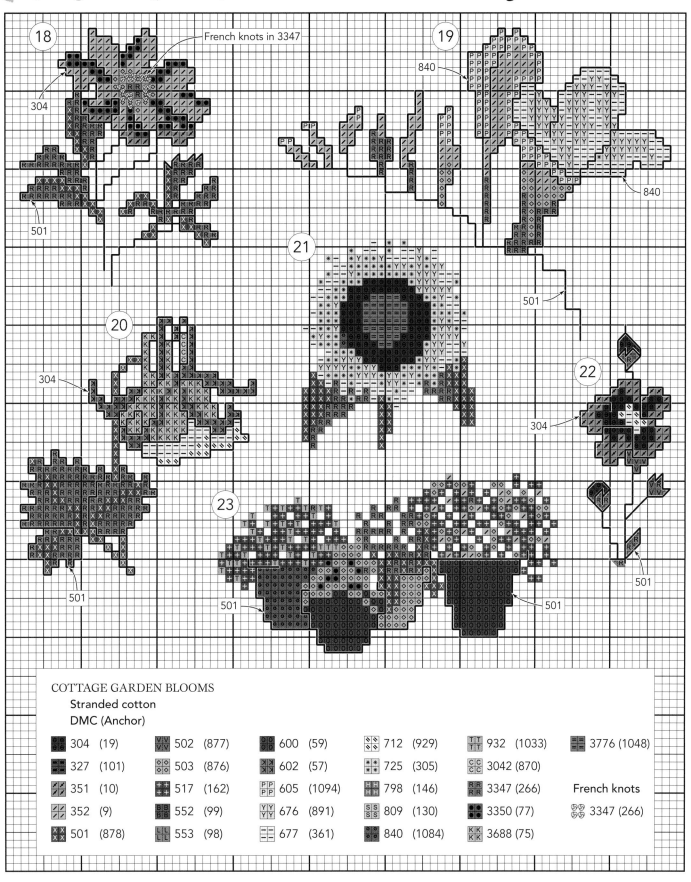

French knots in 3347

304

501

840

840

501

304

501

304

501

501

501

COTTAGE GARDEN BLOOMS
Stranded cotton
DMC (Anchor)

304 (19)	502 (877)	600 (59)	712 (929)	932 (1033)	3776 (1048)
327 (101)	503 (876)	602 (57)	725 (305)	3042 (870)	
351 (10)	517 (162)	605 (1094)	798 (146)	3347 (266)	French knots
352 (9)	552 (99)	676 (891)	809 (130)	3350 (77)	3347 (266)
501 (878)	553 (98)	677 (361)	840 (1084)	3688 (75)	

Thou cannot stir a flower
Without troubling a star.

(Francis Thompson)

Wonderful Wildflowers

To see a world in a grain of sand, And heaven in a wild flower,
Hold infinity in the palm of your hand, And eternity in an hour.

(William Blake)

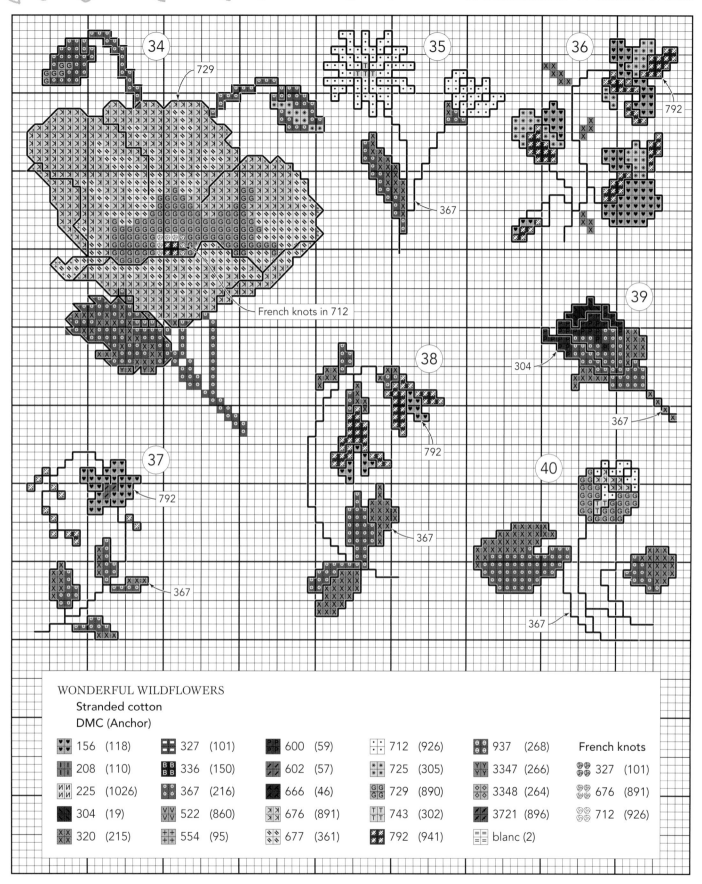

34

35

36
792

729

French knots in 712

367

39
304

367

38
792

37
792

367

40

367

367

WONDERFUL WILDFLOWERS
Stranded cotton
DMC (Anchor)

156 (118)	327 (101)	600 (59)
208 (110)	336 (150)	602 (57)
225 (1026)	367 (216)	666 (46)
304 (19)	522 (860)	676 (891)
320 (215)	554 (95)	677 (361)

		French knots
712 (926)	937 (268)	
725 (305)	3347 (266)	327 (101)
729 (890)	3348 (264)	676 (891)
743 (302)	3721 (896)	712 (926)
792 (941)	blanc (2)	

Roses red and violets blew,
And all the sweetest flowers that in the forrest grew.
(Edmund Spenser)

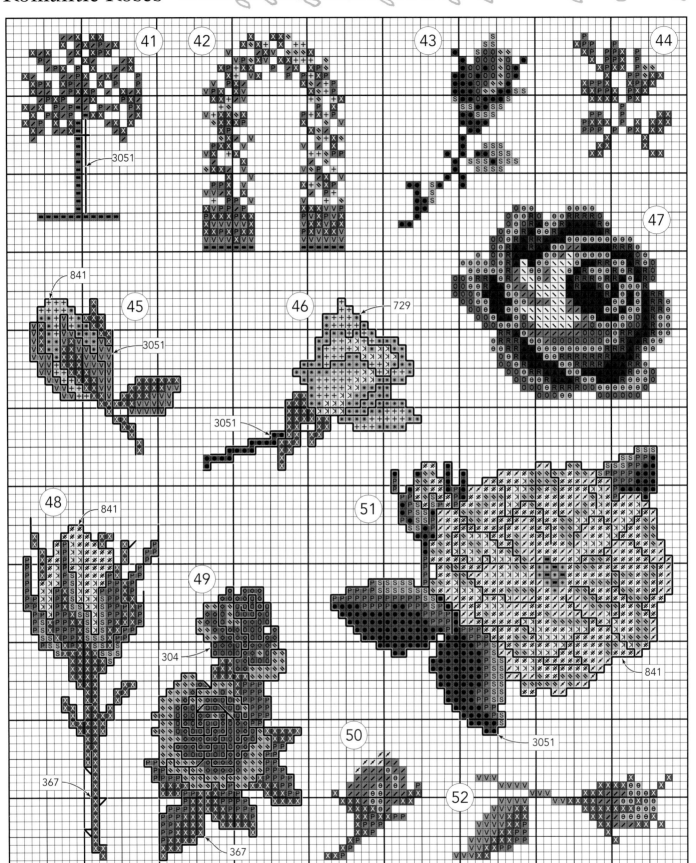

The red rose whispers of passion, And the white rose breathes of love;
O, the red rose is a falcon, And the white rose is a dove.

(John Boyle O'Reilly)

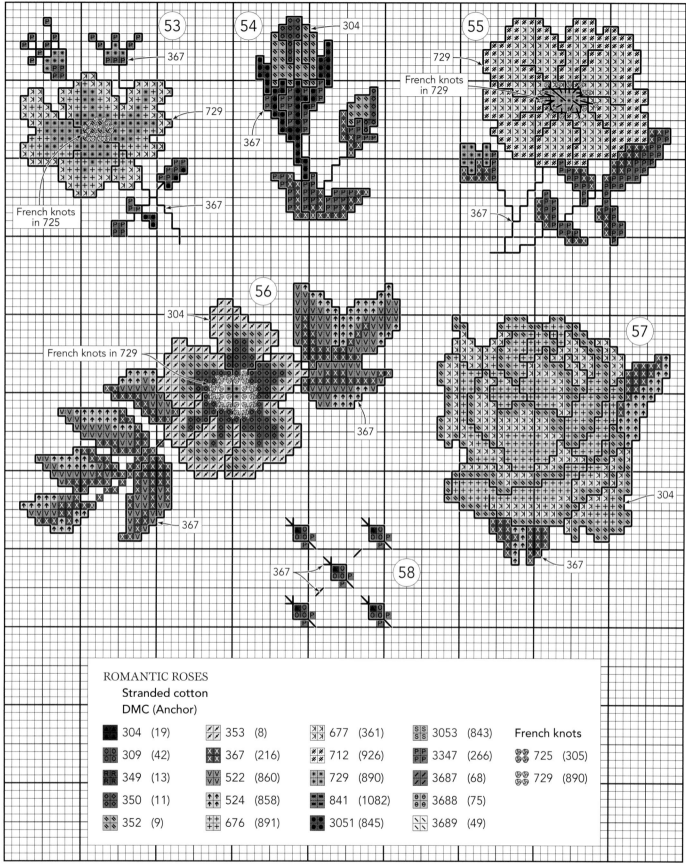

ROMANTIC ROSES
Stranded cotton
DMC (Anchor)

				French knots
304 (19)	353 (8)	677 (361)	3053 (843)	725 (305)
309 (42)	367 (216)	712 (926)	3347 (266)	729 (890)
349 (13)	522 (860)	729 (890)	3687 (68)	
350 (11)	524 (858)	841 (1082)	3688 (75)	
352 (9)	676 (891)	3051 (845)	3689 (49)	

God gave us our memories
so that we might have roses in December.

(J. M. Barrie)

'Tis my faith that every flower
Enjoys the air it breathes.
(William Wordsworth)

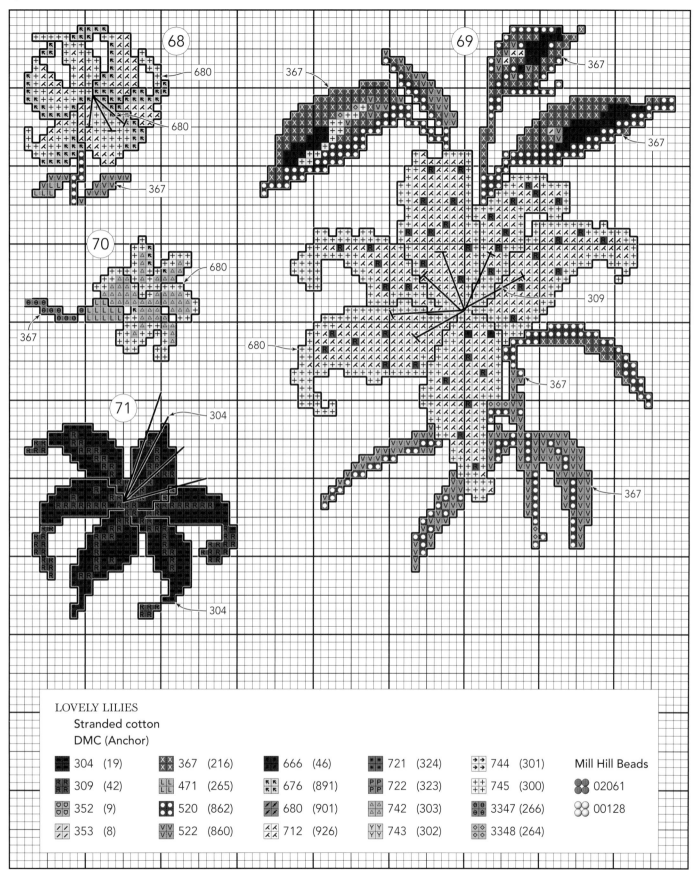

LOVELY LILIES
Stranded cotton
DMC (Anchor)

304 (19)	367 (216)	666 (46)
309 (42)	471 (265)	676 (891)
352 (9)	520 (862)	680 (901)
353 (8)	522 (860)	712 (926)

	Mill Hill Beads
721 (324)	744 (301)
722 (323)	745 (300)	02061
742 (303)	3347 (266)
743 (302)	3348 (264)	00128

Flowers never emit so sweet and strong a fragrance as before a storm.
When a storm approaches thee, be as fragrant as a sweet-smelling flower.
(Jean Paul Richter)

Oriental Orchids

A bit of fragrance clings
to the hand that gives flowers.

(Chinese Proverb)

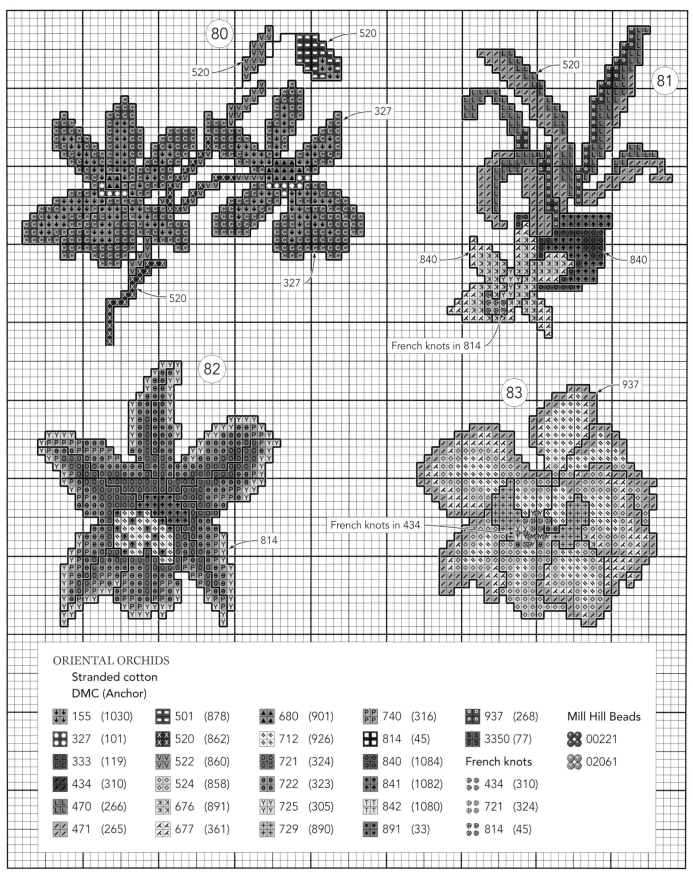

80

520

520

327

520

327

81

520

840

840

French knots in 814

82

83

937

Y Y Y

French knots in 434

814

ORIENTAL ORCHIDS

Stranded cotton
DMC (Anchor)

155	(1030)	501	(878)	680	(901)	740	(316)	937	(268)
327	(101)	520	(862)	712	(926)	814	(45)	3350	(77)
333	(119)	522	(860)	721	(324)	840	(1084)		
434	(310)	524	(858)	722	(323)	841	(1082)		
470	(266)	676	(891)	725	(305)	842	(1080)		
471	(265)	677	(361)	729	(890)	891	(33)		

Mill Hill Beads

00221

02061

French knots

434 (310)

721 (324)

814 (45)

I'd be a butterfly born in a bower,
Where roses and lilies and violets meet.

(Thomas Haynes Bayly)

When you have only two pennies left in the world,
Buy a loaf of bread with one and a lily with the other.

(Chinese Proverb)

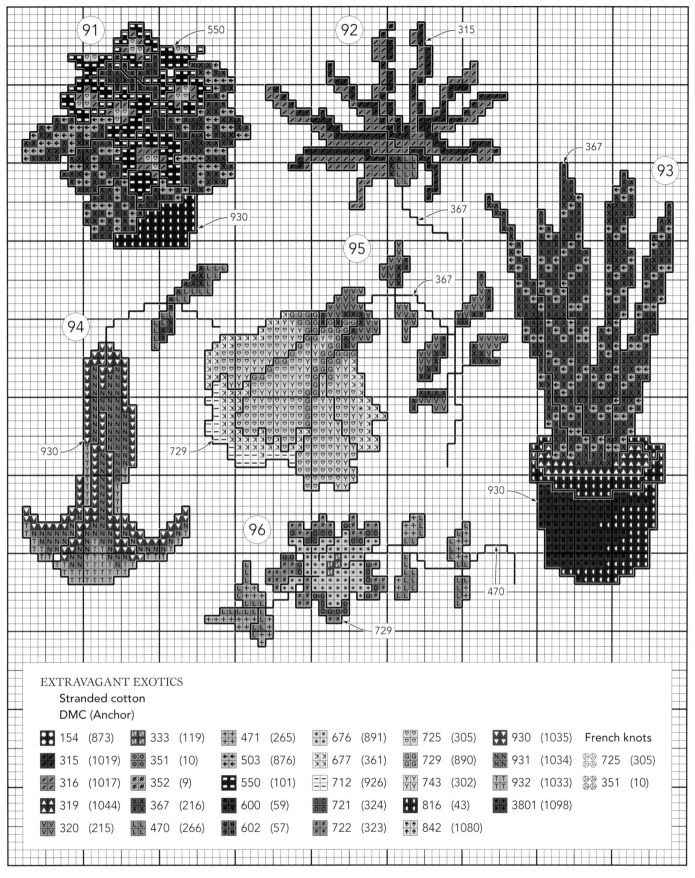

EXTRAVAGANT EXOTICS
Stranded cotton
DMC (Anchor)

154 (873)	333 (119)	471 (265)	676 (891)	725 (305)	930 (1035) French knots
315 (1019)	351 (10)	503 (876)	677 (361)	729 (890)	931 (1034) 725 (305)
316 (1017)	352 (9)	550 (101)	712 (926)	743 (302)	932 (1033) 351 (10)
319 (1044)	367 (216)	600 (59)	721 (324)	816 (43)	3801 (1098)
320 (215)	470 (266)	602 (57)	722 (323)	842 (1080)	

Earth laughs in flowers.
(Ralph Waldo Emerson)

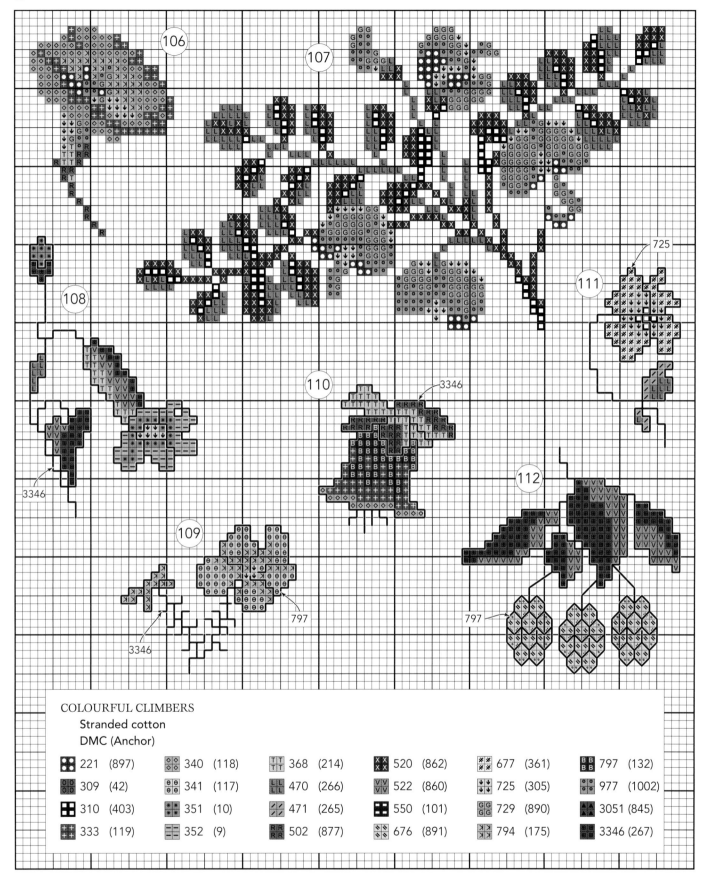

COLOURFUL CLIMBERS
Stranded cotton
DMC (Anchor)

221 (897)	340 (118)	368 (214)	520 (862)	677 (361)	797 (132)
309 (42)	341 (117)	470 (266)	522 (860)	725 (305)	977 (1002)
310 (403)	351 (10)	471 (265)	550 (101)	729 (890)	3051 (845)
333 (119)	352 (9)	502 (877)	676 (891)	794 (175)	3346 (267)

If you would be happy all your life,
plant a garden.

(Anon)

Flowers bring to a liberall and gentlemanly mind the rememberance
of honestie, comeliness and all kinds of virtues.

(John Gerard)

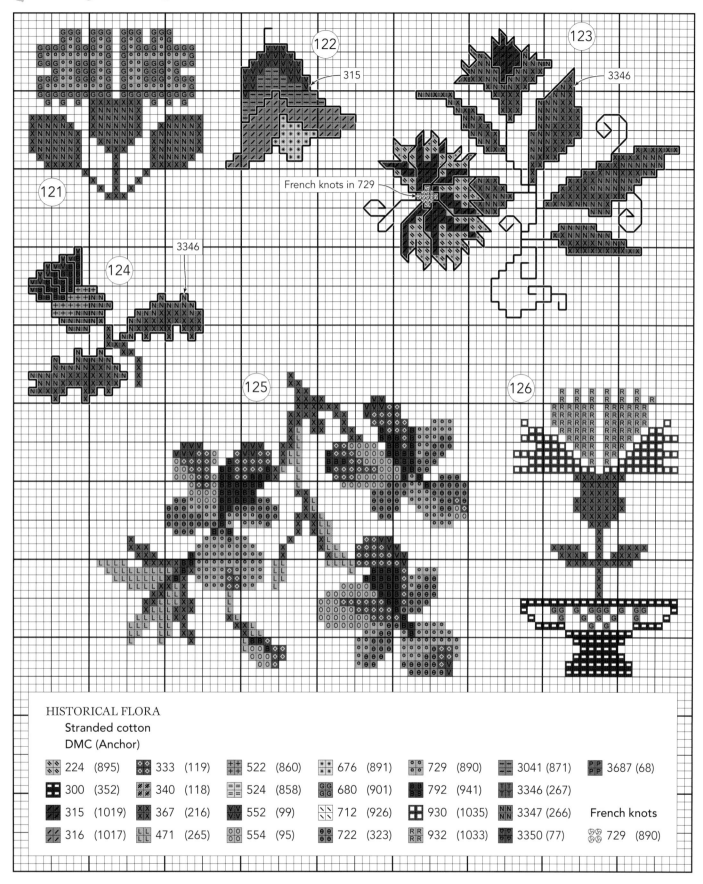

315

French knots in 729

3346

3346

HISTORICAL FLORA
Stranded cotton
DMC (Anchor)

224 (895)	333 (119)	522 (860)	676 (891)	729 (890)	3041 (871)	3687 (68)
300 (352)	340 (118)	524 (858)	680 (901)	792 (941)	3346 (267)	
315 (1019)	367 (216)	552 (99)	712 (926)	930 (1035)	3347 (266)	French knots
316 (1017)	471 (265)	554 (95)	722 (323)	932 (1033)	3350 (77)	729 (890)

The love of gardening is a seed that once sown, never dies.
(Gertrude Jekyll)

Blackwork Patterns

For the adventurous among you, why not use the blackwork and darning patterns here to create your own designs? Alternatively, you could use them to replace patterns used in the book.

One is nearer God's heart in a garden,
than anywhere else on earth.
(Dorothy F. B. Gurney)

Gardens are not made
by sitting in the shade.
(Rudyard Kipling)

Alphabets and Numbers

The alphabets and numbers charted here will help you to customize your designs and make the gifts and cards you create even more special. Change the colours to suit your project. When adding names, dates or messages to a cross stitch design, it is wise to plan it on squared graph paper first, to ensure that the letters or numbers fit the space available. If space is tight, remember that backstitch lettering can be worked over just one thread of an evenweave fabric. You could use the little floral borders and frames charted opposite to decorate your messages or combine them with motifs from the Motif Library to create your own unique designs.

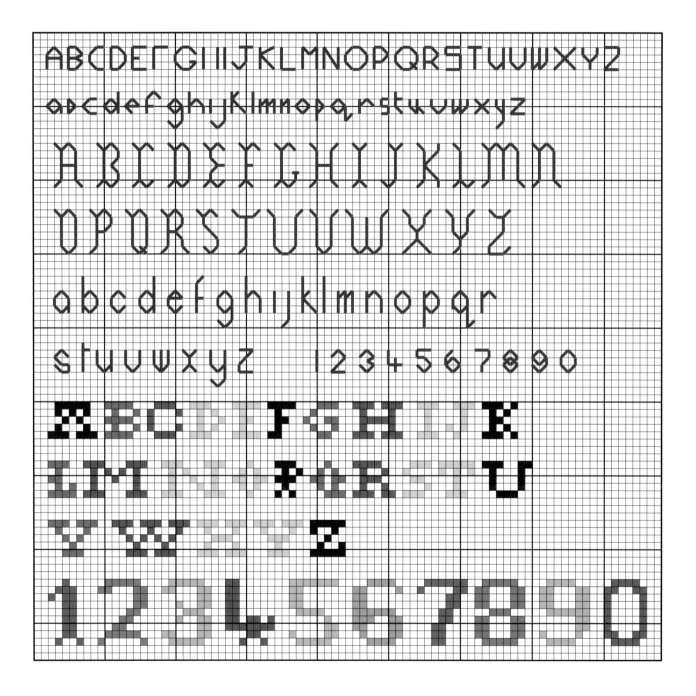

All the flowers of all the tomorrows
are in the seeds of today.
(Indian proverb)

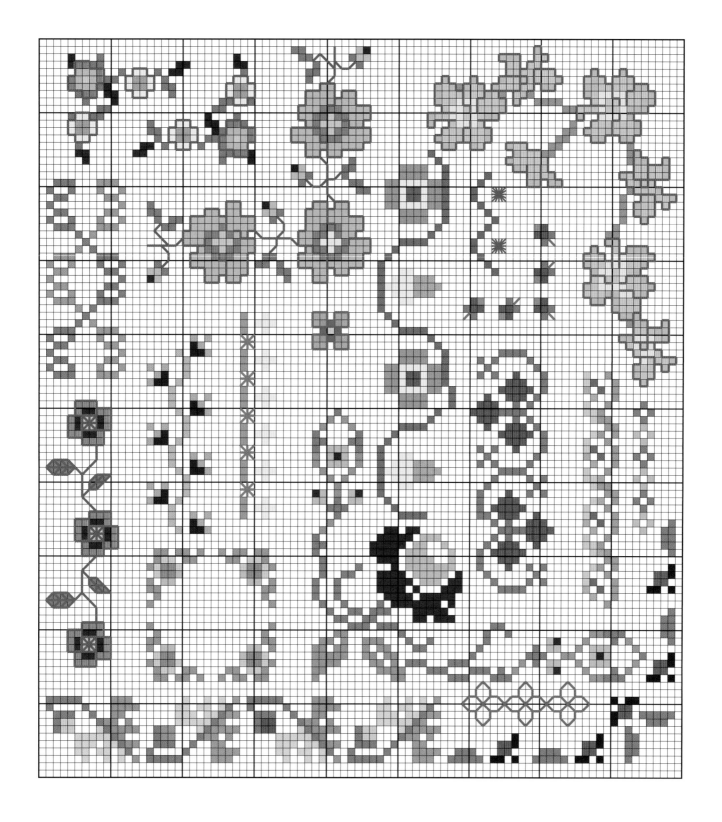

In the hope of reaching the moon
men fail to see the flowers that blossom at their feet.
(Albert Schweitzer)

Stitch Library

The stitches used in this book are described here alphabetically. In many cases stitches may be worked on Aida, evenweave or canvas unless stated otherwise, although I would not recommend working pulled stitches on Aida. I find it useful to have a scrap of 20-count fabric at hand to practise new stitches on before working them on a project. Some of the diagrams show the stitch worked over two or four fabric threads. Many diagrams have a numbered stitching sequence. When working a stitch, the construction stays the same but the size and number of fabric threads used may alter, so refer to the project for the correct number of fabric threads involved. When constructing a stitch, remember which way you worked and keep all the stitches the same, clockwise or anticlockwise. See Back to Basics on page 8 for how to work cross stitch.

Algerian Eye

This pretty star-shaped stitch is a pulled stitch, which means that when it is formed correctly holes are pulled in the fabric. It can be worked over two or four threads of evenweave and is more successful worked on evenweave than Aida.

1 Start to the left of a vertical thread and work from left to right around each stitch in an anticlockwise direction (or vice versa but keeping each stitch the same).

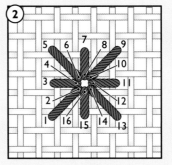

2 Always work an Algerian eye by passing the needle down through the central hole, pulling quite firmly so that a small hole is formed in the centre. Take care that trailing threads do not cover this hole as you progress to the next stitch.

Jane's Tip

If you should prick yourself and get blood on your stitching, act quickly: dampen the spot with your own saliva, press with a tissue and the stain will miraculously disappear!

Backstitch

Backstitch is used for outlining a design or part of a design, to add detail or emphasis, or for lettering. It is usually indicated on a chart by solid lines with the shade code given on the chart or in the key. It is added after the cross stitch has been completed, to prevent the backstitch line being broken by the cross stitches.

To work backstitch, follow the numbered sequence in the diagram, working stitches over one block of Aida or two threads of evenweave, unless stated otherwise on the chart. Avoid using long, loose stitches unless working flower stamens and so on.

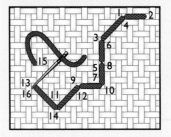

Beads

Working with beads is great fun and easy; because you are working with one colour thread you need not work blocks of colour as for cross stitch but just work across the pattern row by row.

Check the size of the beads you plan to use with your fabric, because if the beads are too large the design will distort and the beads will crowd on top of each other. A rough guide is that most seed beads are perfect for 14-count fabric or canvas.

Attach seed beads and bugle beads with a beading needle or a very fine 'sharp' needle using a half cross stitch and thread that matches the fabric background. Bugles make excellent flower stamens and, because they are longer, are best attached after the cross stitch is completed.

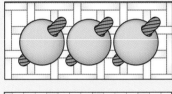

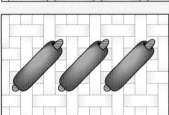

Braided Cross Stitch

This pretty, modern stitch is worked using two strands of stranded cotton (floss) over eight threads and is always square when completed.

Start the stitch from the bottom left and cross to the top right corner. Work two further long stitches as shown in the diagram. Now change direction and work three more long stitches, following the numbered sequence and weaving in and out of the first stitches.

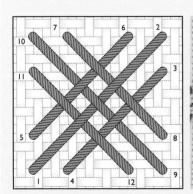

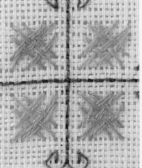

Bullion Stitch

This is a very versatile stitch usually called a knot or bar, which can be formed in straight bars or in curves to form flowers.

1 A straight bullion bar is begun by working an incomplete backstitch, leaving the needle in the fabric. It is vital that the point of the needle exits from the hole where it started.

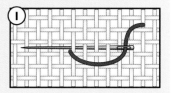

2 With the needle still in the fabric, wind the thread around the needle as many times as necessary to make the coil the length of the incomplete backstitch.

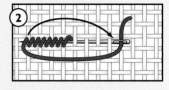

Hold the needle and coil of thread firmly against the fabric, then gently pull the needle through the coil and fabric. Using a gold-plated needle makes this exercise much simpler. To finish the stitch turn the coil back on itself and push the needle through the fabric at the rear of the backstitch.

This thistle from the Wildflower Charm Sampler uses velvet stitch to create a fluffy head, with massed bullion knots for the base

Jane's Tip

Using a gold-plated tapestry needle is very helpful when forming French knots and bullion knots, as the knots will slip into place more easily than with standard nickel-plated needles.

Buttonhole Stitch

This old stitch is simple to work and extremely versatile.

Start with an away waste knot (page 8) and follow the numbered sequence in this diagram. Buttonhole stitches are usually worked closely together but may be spaced more widely according to the pattern you are working.

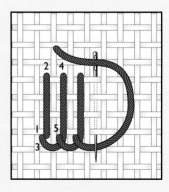

Button Loop

To create a button loop, useful for fastening needlecases, work four straight stitches in and out of the same hole and then bring the needle to the surface at one end. Working on top of the fabric and just under the straight stitches, work buttonhole stitches all along the bar, closely together.

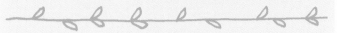

Couching

This is not a counted stitch as such but can be very effective, particularly on a band sampler. Couching is often worked with a metallic thread laid on the fabric, held down by small vertical stitches. Start by bringing the laid thread up through the fabric and laying it across the fabric. Using the couching thread, work small vertical stitches, as shown.

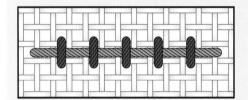

Cross Stitch

Refer to page 8 of Back to Basics for working full cross stitch and three-quarter cross stitch on Aida and evenweave.

Double Cross Stitch

Double cross stitch can be worked over two or four threads of an evenweave fabric or over one or two blocks of Aida, to create a series of bold crosses or stars. Tiny double cross stitches may be formed over two threads of evenweave but they are difficult to work on one block of Aida. To keep all double cross stitches uniform make sure that the direction of the stitches within them is the same.

To work, start to the left of a vertical thread and following the numbered sequence in the diagram, work a diagonal cross stitch and then add a vertical cross on top. The second vertical cross may be worked in a different colour to add interest, in which case work the stitch in two stages – all lower crosses first, followed by the top crosses.

Dove's Eye Stitch

This is a traditional Hardanger stitch usually constructed whilst needleweaving or wrapping. It is used in the Hardanger Tulip Bowl (see picture detail below).

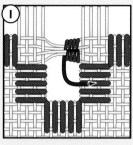

1 Whilst working the last side of a square, needleweave to the centre of the bar, bringing the needle out through a void area.

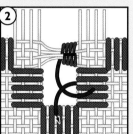

2 Pierce the neighbouring needlewoven bar (or wrapped thread) halfway along its length, bringing the needle up through the void and through the loop formed by the thread.

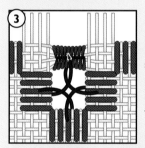

3 Continue round the square following the diagram sequence but before resuming needleweaving, loop the needle under the first stitch to form the final twist in the dove's eye.

Here, dove's eye stitches are worked with needlewoven bars in the Hardanger Tulip Bowl. The Kloster blocks are worked in a variegated thread

Corner Dove's Eye

This filling stitch is added in the same way as a dove's eye stitch above but here the stitch is created by working from each corner of the square. Referring to the diagram, follow the route taken by the needle remembering the last twist to complete the square.

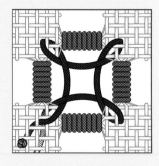

Four-Sided Stitch

This is traditionally worked as a pulled stitch to create a lacy effect without the removal of fabric threads. It can also be used as a hemstitch when threads are to be cut or removed.

The secret of creating a perfect four-sided stitch is to make sure that your needle travels in the correct direction on the back of the stitch. The stitches on the front should be vertical or horizontal but diagonal on the back. It is this tension that forms the small holes as the stitch is worked. The stitch is not recommended for Aida fabric.

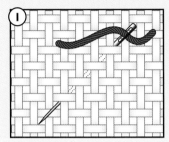

1 Begin to the left of a vertical thread and work a horizontal straight stitch across four threads (or the number indicated on the chart), passing the needle diagonally across four threads at the back of the work.

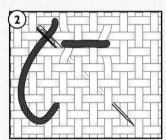

2 Bring the needle up and form a vertical straight stitch, again passing the needle diagonally across four threads at the back of the work.

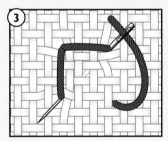

3 Bring the needle up and form another vertical straight stitch, again passing the needle diagonally across four threads at the back.

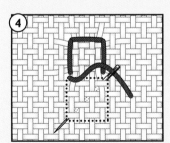

4 Work a horizontal straight stitch to form the last side of the square but this time pass the needle across diagonally to begin the next four-sided stitch.

French Knot

French knots are small but important stitches, though they can cause distress as they are apt to disappear to the back of the work or end up as a row of tiny knots on the thread in the needle! Follow the steps below for perfect knots.

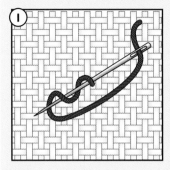

1 Bring the needle through to the front of the fabric and wind the thread around the needle twice. Begin to 'post' the needle partly through to the back, one thread or part of a block away from the entry point (to stop the stitch being pulled to the wrong side).

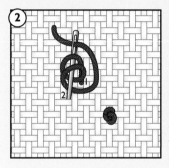

2 Gently pull the thread you have wound so it sits snugly at the point where the needle enters the fabric. Pull the needle through to the back and you should have a perfect knot in position. If you want bigger knots, add more thread to the needle as this gives a better result than winding more times round the needle.

Half Rhodes Stitch with Bar

This is an adaptation of Rhodes stitch (see page 109), producing a decorative stitch shaped rather like a sheaf of corn, with a straight bar across the centre to tie the threads together.

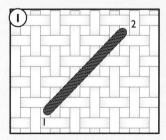

1 Work over squares of two, four, six or eight threads of evenweave fabric in a slanting, anticlockwise direction.

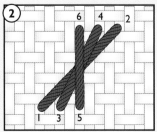

2 Complete the half Rhodes stitch and maintain the same sequence for every stitch to achieve a uniform effect. (Continue overleaf)

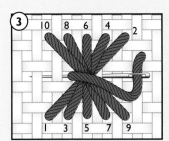

3 To finish, add a single straight stitch across the centre, holding the threads firmly. Buttonhole stitching could be added to the bar for further decoration.

Hemstitch

Hemstitch is wonderfully versatile, allowing you to hem raw edges, form folded hems (see right) or remove horizontal threads and decorate the verticals in various ways. When working hemstitches for the first time it is simple to work them without removing threads first, eliminating the anxiety of cutting too many, although traditionally the threads are removed before the hemstitching. When you have perfected the stitch you can experiment with thread removal – see withdrawing and reweaving threads, which follows.

A hemstitch is made up of parts – two straight stitches and one diagonal on the back. It is this combination that forms the safe barrier if threads are to be cut or removed. If you are intending to cut to the edge, you may prefer to use double hemstitch where each stage of the stitch is worked twice. Hemstitch can look very effective worked in rows without any threads removed. The stitch is not suitable for Aida.

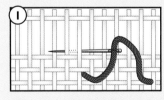

1 This hemstitching is over two threads in each direction. Work a straight stitch across two threads, turning the needle to face horizontally.

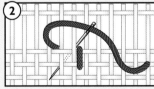

2 Make another straight stitch across two threads, at right angles to the first, then pass the needle down diagonally under two threads.

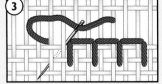

3 Repeat the straight stitches along the row, counting carefully.

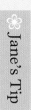
Withdrawing and Reweaving Threads

To remove horizontal threads prior to hemstitching, count carefully to the centre of the band and cut horizontal threads down the centre line (refer to the chart for how many threads to cut). Using a needle, un-pick the linen threads back to the edge of the band. Working in pairs, remove one thread completely and then reweave the other into the gap (see ladder hemstitch, page 108). Continue until all the threads are removed or rewoven. Following the instructions on the chart, hemstitch the remaining fabric threads using two strands of stranded cotton (floss).

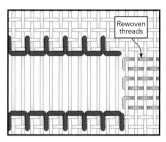

Rewoven threads

Stitching a Folded Hem

Many projects, especially table linen, are beautifully finished off by a folded and stitched hem – see the little needlecase on page 13.

1 From the middle of the long side (of a sampler) count five threads out from the edge of the stitching and cut the sixth thread. Unravel this thread back to the corner and reweave it into the margin. Repeat on all four sides. Now lay the fabric wrong side up on a hard surface and count out from the missing thread to the ninth and tenth threads. Place a tapestry needle between these threads and pull the fabric (not the needle) to score a line and form a crease – this will form the fold at the edge of the work. Repeat on all four sides.

2 Score the fabric again, nine threads further out (line 2 on diagram below). Score another line seven threads out and cut the fabric carefully following this line of threads.

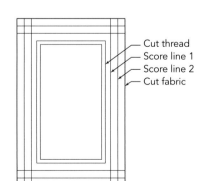

— Cut thread
— Score line 1
— Score line 2
— Cut fabric

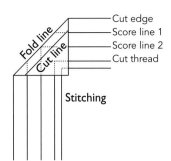

Cut edge
Score line 1
Score line 2
Cut thread

Fold line
Cut line

Stitching

3 Fold the fabric piece at the corners and cut as shown in diagram, left. Now fold in all the edges, mitring the corners.

4 Hemstitch the folded edge in place as shown in the diagram below, at the corners stitching the mitres with invisible stitching up the seam.

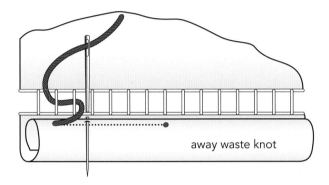

away waste knot

Holbein Stitch

This stitch, also called double running stitch, is the traditional stitch for creating blackwork patterns, which should look the same on the back and front. If backstitch is used instead it creates a rather padded and untidy reverse. Holbein stitch can be worked in two colours by changing colour before completing the gaps on the return journey.

Work a row of running stitch in one direction, counting to ensure that you work under and over two threads of evenweave or one Aida block, and then back over the row in the opposite direction, filling in the gaps.

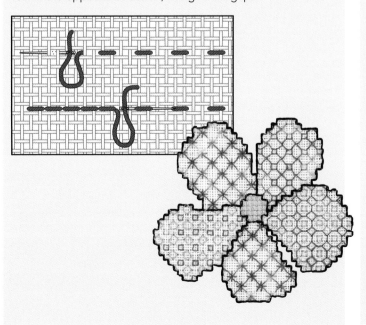

Kloster Blocks

Hardanger embroidery is a type of counted embroidery distinguished by its cutwork and Kloster blocks form the framework for these cut areas. Start with an away waste knot – you will need to be able to snip off the knot and thread the needle with the away knot thread, so allow enough thread.

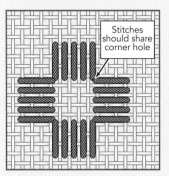

Stitches should share corner hole

1 Kloster blocks are worked in patterns, with 5 vertical or 5 horizontal straight stitches, each of them over 4 threads on evenweave or 4 blocks if working on Hardanger fabric. Keep checking that the blocks are directly opposite each other. The vertical and horizontal blocks must meet at the corners and share the same corner hole. If the stitches are worked side by side they will look the same on the wrong side of the fabric. Make sure that you do not travel between Kloster blocks at the back, unless under existing blocks. Avoid the red route shown in the diagram below.

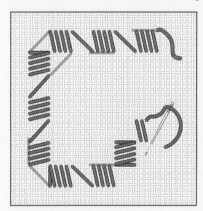

2 When all the blocks are complete and match everywhere, use sharp, pointed scissors to cut across the ends of the blocks. Take this slowly, counting and cutting only two threads each time. Make sure that you can see both scissor points before cutting.

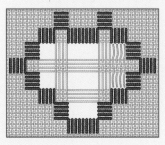

3 Once the threads are cut, withdraw them, leaving the cutwork area ready for needleweaving, wrapped bars and filling stitches.

Ladder Hemstitch

This is the simplest decorative hemstitch. Cut the horizontal threads (see withdrawing and reweaving threads, page 106) and reweave them, as shown. Work two rows of hemstitch as described on page 106 – the vertical threads that remain form a ladder pattern.

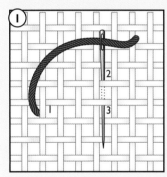

Rewoven threads

Long-Legged Cross Stitch

This stitch looks wonderful when worked in rows because it forms a plaited effect, ideal for borders or for the outside edges of pieces to be made up as a pincushion or a scissor keeper. It can be worked on Aida across two blocks and upwards over one. The stitch can also be used to join sections of stitching together.

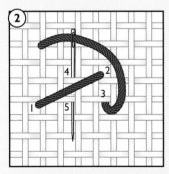

1 To work long-legged cross stitch on evenweave, begin to the left of a vertical thread. Following the number sequence, insert the needle four threads forwards and two threads upwards in a long diagonal 'leg'.

2 Insert the needle two threads upwards and two threads backwards diagonally to make the short leg.

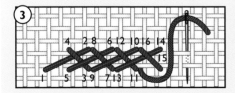

3 To work a row of long-legged cross stitch, follow the numbered sequence here.

Needleweaving

Needleweaving is used to decorate the loose threads that remain either when threads are cut as in Hardanger embroidery or when areas have had threads removed. The needleweaving creates covered bars and these can be decorated with stitches, such as picots, while the spaces between bars can be filled with decorative stitches such as dove's eyes and spider's webs.

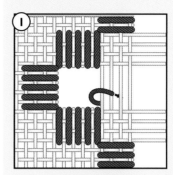

1 Start by anchoring the thread under adjacent cross stitch or hemstitch on the back of the work.

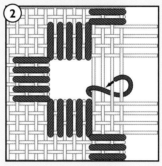

2 Beginning from a cut area, bring the needle up through a void area.

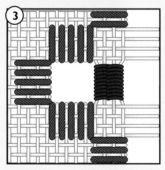

3 Weave the needle under and over pairs of threads to form a plaited effect. The stitches should not distort or bend the threads.

Corner Needleweaving

Corner needleweaving is usually combined with wrapped bars and can look very effective when used in groups. Use an away waste knot and start by wrapping a pair of threads until you are a few stitches away from an intersection. Needleweave the wrapped bar and the bar running at right angles for a few stitches then continue with the wrapping. Keep a record of how many weaves you work so that they all look the same.

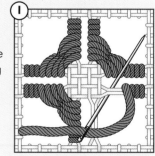

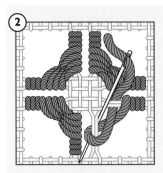

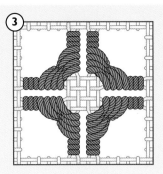

The Hardanger Tulip Bowl features some corner needleweaving and wrapped bars, with needleweaving seen at the outer edges of this detail picture

Pulled Satin Stitch

Pulled satin stitch is worked in the same way as normal satin stitch (page 110) but the threads are pulled as you stitch, which forms holes in the fabric and creates a lacy effect.

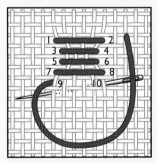

Queen Stitch

This stitch is made of four parts and forms little dimples in the embroidery by pulling small holes in the fabric. It is gorgeous when worked as a group. The stitch is traditionally worked from right to left, but if you find this difficult to count, work the two middle parts first followed by the outer ones.

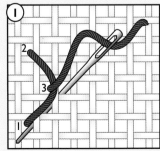

1 Work one long stitch over four threads of the fabric, which is then moved two threads to the right by the needle coming up at 3 and a small stitch worked across one thread.

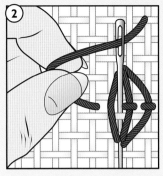

2 Repeat the long stitch from the same position as in the first diagram, but this time bending the stitch over one thread only.

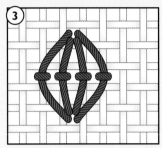

3 Repeat the long stitch from the same position as in the first diagram, but this time the long stitch is bent to the left and the needle re-enters the fabric in the centre position.

4 The last stage of the stitch is completed, forming a lantern shape on the fabric. Note how the top and bottom hole is shared by each stage of the stitch, so forming the holes or little dimples that make this stitch distinctive.

Jane's Tip

Queen stitch is not difficult but is a bit of a brute to unpick so it's worth practising on large-count fabric first. It is a pulled stitch and should be pulled firmly.

Rhodes Stitch

Rhodes stitch produces a solid, slightly raised, three-dimensional effect, almost like a series of studs on the fabric. The diagrams below illustrate one version but the size of the stitch can be altered – check the chart to see how many threads are in each stitch. This stitch doesn't work well on Aida fabric. (See also half Rhodes stitch with a bar on page 105.)

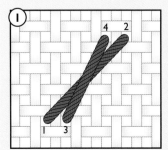

1 Begin to the left of a vertical evenweave thread, working each stitch over squares of two, four or more threads.

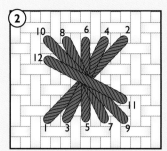

2 Following the numbered sequence, build up the stitch, working in an anticlockwise direction around the square.

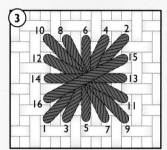

3 A completed Rhodes stitch should have a raised central area. Maintain the same sequence for every Rhodes stitch to produce a uniform effect.

This detail from the Wildflower Stitch Sampler shows Rhodes stitch as the centre cross, surrounded by Algerian eyes and double cross stitch

Rice Stitch

Rice stitch is a cross stitch with an additional stitch worked over each 'leg' or corner of the cross. It can be worked in two stages: a row of normal cross stitches, followed by the additional stitches as a second row. This makes it ideal for working in two colours, which can create very pretty effects. When using two colours, work all large crosses first, followed by the additional stitches in the second colour. Rice stitch is worked over an even number of threads, usually over four threads of an evenweave fabric but it can also be worked to occupy the space of four blocks of Aida. Do not pull the stitch as this will form holes around the edge.

To work rice stitch, start to the left of a vertical thread, working a half cross stitch across four evenweave threads, then returning to complete the cross. In the second diagram additional stitches have been added in another colour. The additional stitches across the legs are traditionally worked as a backstitch into the central side hole in each case.

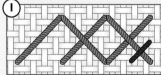 

Satin Stitch

This long stitch is often used to fill shapes and looks very effective when worked in blocks facing in different directions. It can be worked diagonally, horizontally or vertically.

To work satin stitch, start with an away waste knot, which reverses the twist on the thread. Beginning to the left of a vertical thread, follow the numbered sequence in the diagram, laying flat stitches side by side. Always come up the same side and down the other, so the back of the fabric is covered and the stitches lie closely and neatly beside each other. Don't pull too tightly (unless working pulled satin stitch – see page 109).

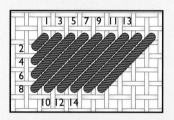

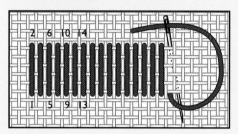

Spider's Web Stitch

This is a traditional filling stitch used to decorate the voids left by cutting threads and is often used with wrapped bars. It is a good idea to keep a note of the number of winds and weaves to ensure the stitches are uniform.

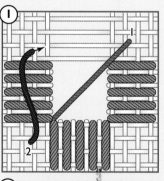

1 Work three sides in Kloster blocks (see page 107), wrapped bars or a combination of both, bringing the needle out at 1. Cross the square bringing the needle out at 2.

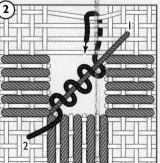

2 Return to position 1, winding the thread around the diagonal just formed, ready to complete the final side (shown as a wrapped bar in the third diagram at the top of page 111).

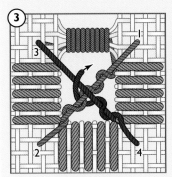

3 Bring the needle up at 3 and pass diagonally to 4, then wind the thread around the diagonal to the centre (as shown in step 2).

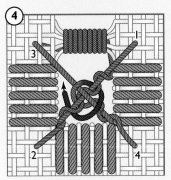

4 Start weaving the spider's web around the diagonals.

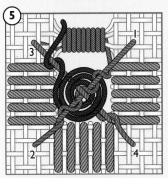

5 After three winds you may need to tighten and adjust the position of the winds to ensure that they are even and in the centre of the square.

6 When the spider's web is complete, leave the stitch by winding around the diagonal as before.

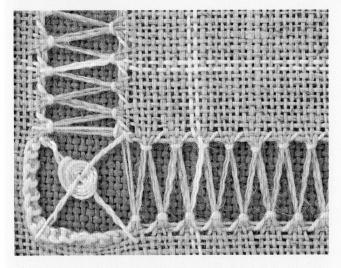

A spider's web stitch worked in the corner of the Hardanger Tulip Bowl picture makes a good companion for the zigzag hemstitch

Velvet Stitch

This is basically a cross stitch with an extra loop in it, left long to create a pile on the fabric. The loops can be left as they are or can all be cut to the same length. Work in rows from bottom to top and left to right.

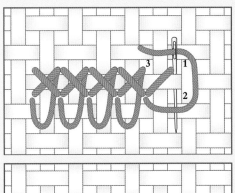

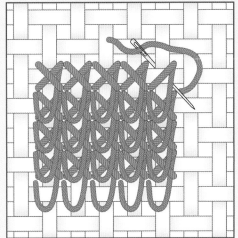

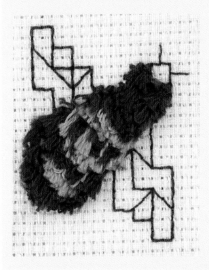

Velvet stitch is quite simple to work and can create a great fun look to your stitching, like this fluffy bumblebee from the card on page 18

Woven Leaf Stitch

This pretty filling stitch can be worked as a leaf shape on the diagonal or as a fan working from the centre of a needlewoven bar. When the framework has been needlewoven, take the thread to the opposite corner and then back to the source. If working across the corner proceed as shown in the diagram. If working a fan take the threads from the centre to the corners and weave as shown.

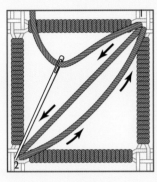
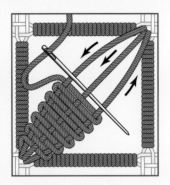

Wrapped Bars

Like needleweaving, wrapped bars may be worked alone to decorate the threads that remain after cutting or withdrawing and as part of other decorative stitches. I've used them with the corner needleweaving in the Hardanger and Tulip Bowl on page 10. The number of wraps will depend on the project – you will need to completely cover the bar when working Hardanger embroidery.

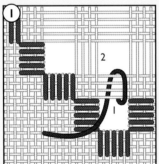

1 Start by anchoring your thread under adjacent hemstitches and then begin wrapping, working horizontally across the fabric.

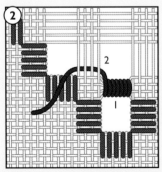

2 Wind the thread around and around the remaining fabric threads, then travel to the next group of threads and repeat. As you wrap each bar hold the threads you are wrapping quite firmly to prevent them unravelling as you work.

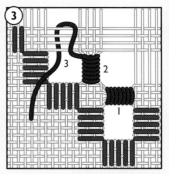

3 Continue wrapping the bars, noting how many times each set is wrapped and keeping the stitches consistent.

Here, wrapped bars lead to a central focus of corner needleweaving

Zigzag Hemstitch

This is formed in almost the same way as ladder hemstitch (page 108). Cut the horizontal threads (see withdrawing and reweaving threads, page 106) and reweave them, as shown. Work one row of hemstitch as for ladder hemstitch and then work the second row but offset the stitches by one fabric thread to create a zigzag effect.

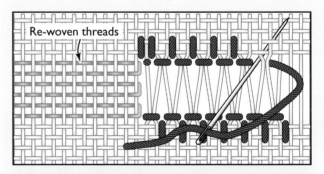

Re-woven threads

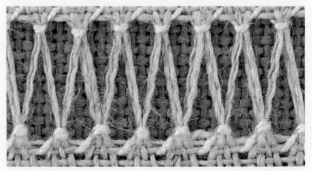

Making Up

How your embroidery is finished and made up makes a great deal of difference to the look of the piece. This section describes some of the finishing techniques used in this book. Unless otherwise stated use 1.25cm (½in) seam allowances. You will need sewing threads to match your embroidery project.

Stretching and Mounting

Your embroidery will look its best if stretched and mounted. When mounting small cards or novelty projects you can use double-sided adhesive tape, but it is worth taking more time and effort on larger projects.

All the framed embroidery in this book has been mounted using polyester wadding (batting) to create a padded finish. The advantage of this for embroidery is that any slightly lumpy bits on the back of your work will be pushed into the padding rather than appear as raised areas on the front. The padding also raises the embroidery up, which displays it to better effect. When pinning your work to a covered board the embroidery must be centred and stretched evenly because any wobbles will show when the design is framed.

To stretch and mount your embroidery you will need either acid-free mounting board or lightweight foam board or foam core, dressmaker's pins and double-sided tape or strong thread if lacing.

1 Using a sharp craft knife cut a piece of foam core board to fit your frame – an easy way to do this is to cut round the piece of glass that fits the frame.

2 Trim the wadding (batting) to the same size as the foam core and attach it to the foam core using strips of double-sided tape. Position your embroidery on top of the padding and centre it carefully in relation to the board. Fix the embroidery in position by pinning through the fabric into the edges of the board. Start in the middle of each side and pin towards the corners, making sure your pins follow a line of Aida holes or a linen thread so that edges will be really straight. If necessary, adjust the fabric's position until it is centred and straight, with no wobbles.

3 Turn the work over, leaving the pins in place, trim the excess fabric to about 5cm (2in) all round. Attach the excess fabric to the back of the board with double-sided tape or lace across from side to side with strong buttonhole thread.

Framing

You will see from some of the wonderful photographs in this book, that the way in which a design is framed can greatly affect the end appearance. Mounting and framing by a professional can be expensive, particularly if you want something a little different, but most of the finishing techniques suggested here can be tackled by the amateur at home, and will save money.

When choosing a frame for a particular project, select the best moulding you can afford. Generally embroidery looks better framed without glass but if you prefer to use glass you must ensure that the embroidery does not get squashed by the underside of the glass. Either use a spacer (narrow strips of board), gold slip, or a mount (mat) between the glass and the mounted embroidery to hold them apart.

To frame your stitching, stretch and mount as described above and set aside. Place the frame face down on a covered surface and after cleaning both sides of the glass, place the glass in the frame rebate and insert the gold slip, mount or spacer, followed by the stitching. Before fixing in the backboard and sealing the frame, line the inside with some aluminium foil, which will discourage thunder flies from finding their way in!

Mounting Work in Cards

There are many card blanks available from needlecraft shops and mail-order companies or you can make your own using pretty papers, card and ribbon, as I have for the Three Orchid Card on page 48. The card shown below features a flowerpot button and motifs from the Spring Flowers Sampler. The finished embroidery is frayed, mounted on to handmade paper and then on to cream card, with a little raffia bow as a finishing touch.

In all cases, cut the finished embroidery to the required size (allowing for fraying the edges if appropriate) and then select a coloured card that complements your project. Create a single-fold card and embellish it with decorative paper. Attach the embroidery to the card with double-sided adhesive tape and add trims or other embellishments as desired.

Making up an Amulet Purse

Many of the designs in the book could be used to decorate a little purse or amulet. The following instructions are for making up the Beaded Clematis Amulet on page 64.

You will need

- The completed embroidery
- 35.5 x 13cm (14 x 5in) matching silk moiré fabric
- Polyester wadding (batting)
- Satin bias binding

1 Place the cross stitch on a clean flat surface and cut a curve to the cross-stitched end of the fabric to make the flap. The edge of a dinner plate will help you draw a perfect curve. Using the embroidery as a template, cut the lining fabric and the polyester wadding to match.

2 Sandwich the cross stitch, wadding and lining fabric together, right sides out and pin carefully. Machine around the edge and trim away any excess.

3 Using the bias binding (to make your own, see page 118), bind the short straight edge that will be the inside of the amulet. Fold the bound edge up to the middle to form the pocket and tack (baste) into position.

4 To make a strap, cut a piece of bias binding 90cm (35in) long and fold in half along the length, wrong sides together. Machine along the length using matching thread. Pin the ends of the strap at right angles to the edge of the amulet at the top of the flap. Tack in position.

5 Now bind up one side all around the flap and down the other side. To attach the bias binding you can either machine first on the wrong side and then top stitch down on the right side, or vice versa.

Making up a Bell Pull

The Jacobean Flower design on page 70 has been made up into a simple but attractive bell pull.

You will need
- The completed embroidery
- Curtain Vilene
- Lining fabric
- Bell pull ends and rod
- Decorative cord

1 Begin by measuring the stitching and, allowing for your preferred margin, select a pair of bell pull ends. The pineapple ends shown in the picture have a wooden rod which can be trimmed to suit the project (see Suppliers).

2 Cut a piece of Vilene and a piece of lining fabric the size of the completed project, allowing 1.25cm (½in) seam allowances. Place the embroidery right side down on a clean, flat surface, centre the Vilene on top and pin in position. Fold in the raw edges of the embroidery and then tack (baste) into position.

3 Fold in the raw edges on the lining fabric and place on the Vilene, covering the back of the embroidery to within 2cm (¾in) from the outer edges. Slipstitch the lining in position down the two long sides.

4 Fold over the top and bottom narrow edges to form a channel for the bell pull rods. Pin in position and slipstitch invisibly. Slide the rods into position at the top and bottom and then add the bell pull ends. Use some decorative cord to hang the bell pull or make a length of twisted cord from matching threads (see page 118).

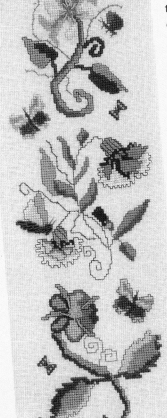

Making up a Glasses Case

The Morning Glory Glasses Case is made in the same way as the Beaded Clematis Amulet but does not have the front flap.

You will need
- The completed embroidery
- Polyester wadding (batting)
- Dark blue satin bias binding

1 Place the cross stitch on a clean flat surface and trim away excess fabric. Using the embroidery as a template, cut lining fabric and polyester wadding to match. Sandwich the cross stitch, wadding and lining fabric together, right sides out and pin carefully. Machine around the edge and trim away any excess.

2 Using the bias binding, bind the two short edges that will be the top of the case. Fold in half matching the two bound edges. Cut a piece of bias binding 120cm (48in) long and pin in position down one side of the case. Now bind up one side, along the edge of the bias binding forming the strap and then down the final side. See page 118 for attaching bias binding.

Making a Simple Cushion

The Clematis Trellis Cushion on page 64 is made up very simply, without a mitred front or any framing fabric.

You will need
- The completed embroidery
- Backing fabric
- Decorative braid
- Cushion pad (pillow)

For a basic cushion (or pincushion), place the embroidered fabric and same size of backing fabric wrong sides together and sew together around all sides, leaving a gap for turning. Turn through to the right side, insert a cushion pad or stuffing and slipstitch the gap closed. The edge can be decorated with twisted cord or braid.

Making a Mitred Cushion

A mitred front to a cushion (pillow) gives it a professional touch and really sets off the embroidery, as you can see by the Antique Flowers Cushion.

You will need
- The completed embroidery
- Backing and border fabric
- Decorative piping
- Cushion pad (pillow)

1 Measure the embroidery and decide on the size the finished cushion is to be. Allow 1.25cm (½in) seam allowances throughout. Subtract the embroidery measurement from the two finished measurements, divide by two and add on the two seam allowances. This gives the total width of the border pieces. The length of the border pieces is the finished measurement of the cushion cover plus two seam allowances.

2 Press the embroidery face down on several soft towels. Cut the linen to the required size plus two seam allowances. Find the mid-point of each edge by folding and mark with a pin. Now fold each border panel in half to find the centre point and mark with a pin. Pin the border panels to the embroidery, matching the centre points and leaving the edges free.

3 Machine stitch these seams around each side of the square. The seams should meet at the corners at right angles. Fold the embroidery in half diagonally, wrong sides together, and mitre the corners by stitching a line from the corner of the embroidery to the corner of the border panels (see diagram). Trim excess fabric and clip corners. Repeat for the remaining corners.

4 The cushion can now be made up in the same way as a simple cushion (page 115), with piping or a decorative cord trimming.

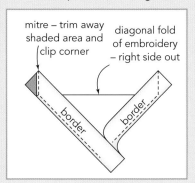

mitre – trim away shaded area and clip corner

diagonal fold of embroidery – right side out

border

border

Making up a Purse

The lovely Passion Flower Purse on page 66 is very simple to make up.

You will need
- The completed embroidery
- 30.5 x 19cm (12 x 7½in) matching silk moiré fabric
- Same size in polyester wadding (batting)

1 Place the cross stitch on a clean, flat surface and use it as a template for cutting a piece of moiré lining fabric and wadding. Only cut enough to line the main purse and not the front flap.

2 Lay the polyester wadding in position on the wrong side of the cross stitch 2cm (¾in) from the straight edge. Fold the raw edge of the fabric over the wadding (batting) and machine across the hem. This forms the top inside edge of the purse. Fold the purse, right sides together and machine up the side seams. Trim the seams and turn the purse through to the right side. At this stage handle it as little as possible to avoid excessive creasing.

3 Fold the lining piece right sides together and machine up each side. Slip the lining bag inside the purse, fold in the raw edges and slipstitch invisibly inside the front hem and along the back of the purse.

Making up a 'Poppet'

This combined scissor and needlecase is a lovely way to display cross stitch embroidery and is also a very functional item.

You will need

- The completed embroidery
- Plain white card
- Cream flannel
- Zweigart Kingston fine linen (shade 222) for linings: one piece 10 x 7.5cm (4 x 3in) two pieces 13 x 18cm (5 x 7in)
- Double-sided tape
- Ecru stranded cotton (floss).

1 Cut two pieces of card, the size as shown in the diagram below. Keep one piece of card until step 2 and use the other piece as a template to cut two pieces of flannel exactly the same size. Using the template again cut two pieces of lining fabric but this time 1cm (⅜in) larger all the way around.

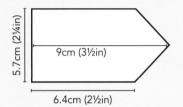

5.7cm (2¼in) 9cm (3½in) 6.4cm (2½in)

2 Using double-sided tape, stick a piece of flannel on one side of each shaped card. Place the stitching on top of the flannel carefully checking the position. Fold excess fabric to the back trimming it if necessary and then hold in position with a little tape.

3 Take one of the 13 x 18cm (5 x 7in) pieces of lining fabric, fold over the top short raw edge and using a sharp needle and matching thread, attach it to the linen by slipstitching. Continue around the shaped section tucking in the raw edges neatly as you go. At this stage you should have a sandwich, as shown in the diagram below. Make up the back shaped section in the same way. Cut the remaining piece of card so that it will fit inside the poppet.

4 Now make a twisted cord, using ecru stranded cotton, following the instructions overleaf.

5 Make up the needle pad as described above using the remaining smaller piece of lining fabric, but slip the knotted end of the twisted cord into the middle of one of the short sides as you slipstitch the sandwich together.

6 To complete the poppet, place the lined sides together and carefully and invisibly stitch down one straight edge and down towards the point. At this stage, insert the needle pad, allowing the cord to hang out through the point and then slipstitch the remaining sides. Check that the needle pad can move in and out of the poppet and that you have not stitched the twisted cord to the poppet.

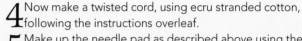

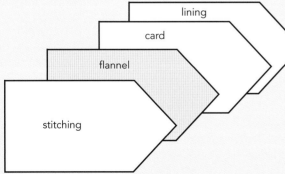

lining
card
flannel
stitching

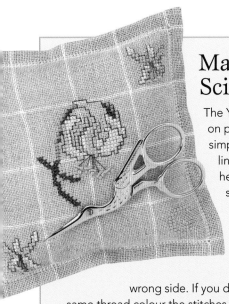

Making a Scissor Pad

The Yellow Lily Scissor Pad on page 40 is made up quite simply. Cut a piece of plain linen the same size as the hemmed square. Place the stitching, right side down on a clean, flat surface and, turning under the raw edges of the cut fabric, slipstitch it to the hemstitches on the wrong side. If you do this neatly and in the same thread colour the stitches will not be visible from the right side. Work around three sides, and then stud the pad with polyester wadding, pushing it into the corners. Push in a strong magnet and slipstitch the last side.

Making a Twisted Cord

A twisted cord is perfect for embellishing all sorts of projects (see the Blue Harebell Poppet, also shown below).

Choose a colour or group of colours in stranded cottons (floss) to match your embroidery. Cut a minimum of four lengths at least four times the finished length required and fold in half. Ask a friend to hold the two ends while you slip a pencil through the loop at the other end. Twist the pencil and continue twisting until kinks appear. Walk slowly towards your partner and the cord will twist. Smooth out the kinks from the looped end and secure with a knot at the other end.

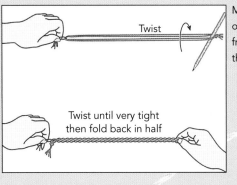

Twist

Twist until very tight then fold back in half

Making a length of twisted cord from embroidery threads

Making Bias Binding

Some of the projects have been completed using purchased satin binding but you can easily make your own.

To make bias binding, cut strips of fabric 4cm (1½in) wide across the grain of the fabric and machine sew them together at 45-degree angles to make the length needed.

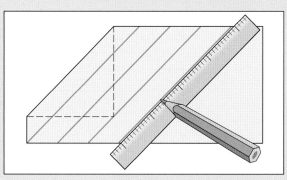

Marking bias strips prior to cutting them

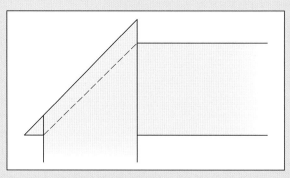

Joining bias strips at a 45-degree angle

To attach bias binding by hand or machine, cut the binding to the correct length and pin it to the wrong side of the project, matching raw edges. Machine or hand stitch in place. Now fold the binding to the right side and top stitch in position. Press lightly.

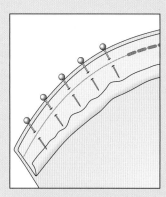

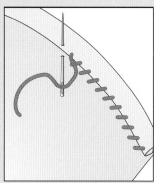

Pinning the binding to the front of the work, ready to machine it in place

Slipstitching the folded edge of the binding to the back of the work

Suppliers

UK

If ringing from outside the UK use
+44 and no (0)

Artistuff Framing Limited
40–41 Fleet Street, Swindon, SN1 1RE
Tel: +44 (0) 1793 522152
*For all the stunning picture frames
used in this book*

Burford Needlecraft
High St, Burford, Oxfordshire
OX18 4RG
Tel: +44 (0) 1993-822136
*For needlework supplies, Caron threads,
pincushion bases and Framecraft
accessories (also mail order)*

The Cross Stitch Guild
Yells Yard, Cirencester Road, Fairford,
Gloucestershire GL7 4BS
Tel: +44 (0) 1285 713799
www.thecrossstitchguild.com
*For a wide range of needlework supplies,
including Zweigart fabrics, threads,
hand-crafted buttons, cross stitch design
software, stitching paper, bell pull ends,
magnets and gold-plated needles*

Coats Crafts UK
PO Box 22, Lingfield Estate, McMullen
Road, Darlington, County Durham,
DL1 1YQ
Tel: +44 (0) 1325 365457
(for a list of stockists)
Fax: +44 (0) 1325 338822
*For a wide range of needlework supplies,
including Anchor threads*

DMC Creative World Ltd
Pullman Road, Wigston, Leicestershire
LE18 2DY
Tel: +44 (0) 116 281 1040
Fax: +44 (0) 116 281 3592
www.dmc.com
*For a wide range of needlework supplies,
including DMC threads and fabrics*

Sue Hawkins Needleworks
East Wing, Highfield House, Whitminster
Gloucestershire GL2 7PJ
Tel: +44 (0) 1452 740118
www.suehawkins.com
For upholstered needlework frames

Heritage Stitchcraft
Redbrook Lane, Brereton, Rugeley,
Staffordshire WS15 1QU
Tel: +44 (0) 1889 575256
Email: enquiries@heritagestitchcraft.com
www.heritagestitchcraft.com
*For Zweigart fabrics and other
embroidery supplies*

The Paper Shed
Tollerton, York YO61 1QQ
Tel: +44 (0) 1347 838253
www.papershed.co.uk
For decorative papers

US

Kreinik Manufacturing Co Inc
3106 Timanus Lane, Suite 101, Baltimore,
Maryland 21244
Tel: 1 800 537 2166 or 1 410 281 0040
Fax: 1 410 281 0987
www.kreinik.com
*For Kreinik metallic threads and
blending filaments*

M & J Buttons
1000 Sixth Avenue, New York NY 10018
Tel: 212 391 6200
www.mjtrim.com
For beads, buttons, ribbons and trimmings

Yarn Tree Designs
PO Box 724, Ames, Iowa 500100724
Tel: 1 800 247 3952
www.yarntree.com
For cross stitch supplies and card mounts

Zweigart/Joan Toggit Ltd
262 Old Brunswick Road, Suite E,
Picataway, NJ 08854-3756
Tel: 732 562 8888
www.zweigart.com
For cross stitch fabrics and linens

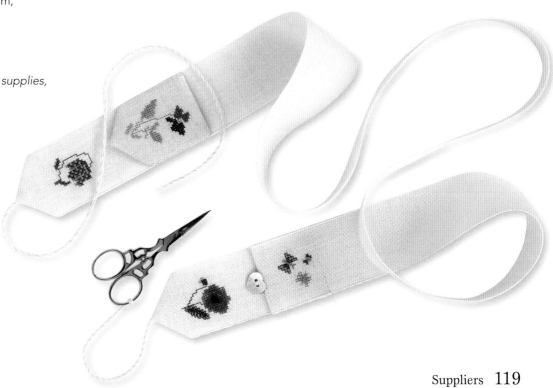

Acknowledgments

I cannot thank my suppliers and contributors enough. Over the past 20 years I have been dealing with many of the people listed below without whom all would grind to a halt! Without the support of my family and my team at The Cross Stitch Guild it would be simply impossible to continue writing cross stitch books. To all the following with love and thanks: Bill, my husband, who continues to accept the household muddle, fast food and too many late nights, and Vivienne Wells who still works tirelessly in the background making sure that *Stitch That*, our CSG magazine, is published on time in spite of everything.

Sue Hawkins who is always at the end of a phone, day and night, and for her friendship, which even survives working together! To my right-hand woman, Helen Beecroft who supports and protects me when scribbling and Daphne and Mina who keep the business going in my absence.

Many thanks to my marvellous team of stitchers and pattern testers: Lesley Clegg, Jill Vaughan, Margaret Cornish, Margaret Pallant, Susan Bridgens, Deborah Buglass, Liz Burford, Jacqueline Davies, Doreen Ely, Elizabeth Edwards, Jean Fox, Joyce Halliday, Joan Hastewell, Janet Jarvis, Mina King, Margaret Locke, Sue Smith, Suzanne Spencer, Joan Barnes, Sue Heeley and Jane King.

To all the team at David & Charles for continuing to put up with me, particularly Cheryl Brown, Jennifer Proverbs and Prudence Rogers. To my editor, the perfectionist Linda Clements, who prevents me making publishing mistakes and does not miss a thing! I must also mention Ethan Danielson who can read my writing and produces all the charts and excellent diagrams that make this book so special.

To Liz Elvin, Principal of the Royal School of Needlework for allowing me access to the archives. Thanks to all the generous suppliers of the materials and equipment required for this book, particularly Rainer Steimann of Zweigart for lovely fabrics, DMC Creative World and Coats Crafts UK for stranded cottons and metallic threads and Ian Lawson Smith for my wonderful cross stitch design programme.

About the Author

Jane Greenoff became interested in counted embroidery when her children were small, now over 20 years ago, and has never looked back. Self taught and a self-confessed stitching addict, Jane has been published 17 times, made two videos and a double DVD. Her book, *The Cross Stitcher's Bible* is available in ten languages and many of her other titles are still in print. She lives in the Cotswolds where she designs and writes, and runs the kit production for The Inglestone Collection. She founded The Cross Stitch Guild and holds classes in her converted barn and also hosts weekend events for Paramount Hotels and the Hilton Group.

The Cross Stitch Guild

The Cross Stitch Guild was formed in March 1996 and quickly became a worldwide organization with a committed and enthusiastic body of members – over 2,000 in the first six months of operation. As word spreads it is clear that many cross stitch and counted thread addicts around the world are delighted to have a Guild of their own. The CSG has received an extraordinary level of support from designers, retailers, manufacturers and stitchers. Guild members receive a full-colour magazine *Stitch That with Jane Greenoff*, including free counted cross stitch designs and technical advice and information. The CSG also supplies cross stitch tours, weekends, cross stitch kits, gold-plated needles, stitchers' gifts and counted thread classes. Taster Membership and Full Membership is available all over the world and there is now a comprehensive website for members and non-members with discounted shopping.

www.thecrossstitchguild.com
For more information and a catalogue contact:
CSG HQ, Yells Yard, Cirencester Road, Fairford, Gloucestershire, GL7 4BS, UK.
Tel: from the UK 0800 328 9750;
from overseas +44 1285 713799.

Index

Stitch instructions indicated by bold

A
Aida 6, 8
Algerian eye stitch 30, **102**
Alphabets 47, 100
Amaryllis, frosted 58–9, 62–3

B
Backstitch 9, **102**
Beads 50, 56, 57–8, 60, 66, **103**
Bell pull, Jacobean flower 70–1, 74–5, 115
Bias binding 118
Blackwork 34–5, 39, 42, 44, 98–9
Blending filaments 48, 58, 62
Book covers 20–1, 70, 74
Borders 9, 101
Bullion stitch 23, 27, 46, 47, 50, 58, 73–5, **103**
Bumblebees 18–19, 22–3
Butterflies 27, 69, 73–5
Buttonhole stitch 67, **103**
Button loop **104**

C
Cards 114
    briar rose 78–9
    fluffy bumblebee 18, 22
    orchid 48, 52, 78–9
    red lily 78–9, 88
    rosebud 32, 36
Charms, and wildflower sampler 26–7
Charts, using 6, 7, 9
Chatelaine, wildflower 24, 27, 28
Clematis 64–5, 69, 114, 115
Climbing plants 64–9, 94–5
Coaster, Hardanger 10, 16–17
Cord, twisted 118
Cottage garden blooms 18–23, 82–3
Couching 104
Cross stitch **8**, 9
    braided 14, **103**
    double **104**
    long-legged 31, **108**
    three-quarter **8**
Cushions
    antique flowers 72–3
    beaded hibiscus 57–8, 61
    clematis trellis 64–5, 69
    making up 115, 116

D
Darning patterns 31, 45, 99
Design size 7
Dove's eye stitch 12, 28, **104**

E
Edges 7, 106
Equipment 6–7
Evenweave 6, 8
Exotic flowers 56–63, 92–3

F
Fabric 6, 7, 8
Finishing work 7, 8, 113–18
Four-sided stitch 30, **105**
Foxglove, garden diary 20–1
Frames/hoops 7
French knot **105**

G
Glasses case, morning glory 68, 115

H
Hardanger **12**, **107**
    coaster 10
    poppy heart 28–9
    tulip bowl 10–12, 16–17
Harebell poppet 26, 31, 117
Hemstitch **106–7**, **108**, **112**
Hibiscus 56–8, 60, 61
Historical flora 70–5, 96–7, 115
Holbein stitch 35, **107**
Hollyhocks 18–19, 22–3
Honeysuckle 70–1, 74–5
Hummingbird 56–7, 60

K
Kloster blocks **12**, 28, 66, **107**

L
Ladder hemstitch **108**
Lilies 40–7, 78–9, 88–9, 118

M
Making up 113–18
Materials 6–7, 119
Measurements 6, 7
Mobile phone case 68
Morning glory, glasses case 68, 115
Motif library 6, 76–101
Mounting work 113–14

N
Needlecase
    blue harebell poppet 26, 31, 117
    Spring flowers 13–14
Needles 6–7, 24
Needleweaving 12, 28, **108–9**
Numbers 100

O
Orchids 48–55, 78–9, 90–1
Outlines 9, 101

P
Pansy 27, 30, 75, 82, 97
Passion flower 66–7, 94, 116
Pincushion
    hummingbird 56, 60
    lilies 78–9
    yellow lily 40, 47
Poppet, blue harebell 26, 31, 117
Poppy, Hardanger heart 28–9
Purse
    beaded clematis 64, 69, 114
    passion flower 66–7, 116

Q
Queen stitch 14, **109**

R
Rhodes stitch 30–1, **109–10**
    half, with bar 31, **105–6**
Rice stitch 30, **110**
Roses 32–9, 78–9, 86–7

S
Samplers
    Spring flowers 13–15
    wildflower 24–5, 26–7, 30–1
Satin stitch 24, **110**
    pulled 30, **109**
Scissors 7, 24
    blue harebell poppet 26, 31, 117
    yellow lily pad 40, 47, 118
Spider's web stitch 28, **110–11**
Spring flowers 10–17, 80–1
Starting work 7–8, 9
Stitch library 6, 102–12
Stretching work 113

T
Thread 6, 9, 58, 62
Trinket pots 52, 78–9, 95
Tulips 10–12, 16–17, 72–3, 80

V
Velvet stitch 18, 27, **111**

W
Washing 7, 102
Wildflowers 24–31, 84–5
Woven leaf stitch 28, **112**
Wrapped bars 12, **112**

Z
Zigzag hemstitch 12, **112**